Praise for *Government Policies and the Delayed Economic Recovery*

This book is a fascinating mix of facts, opinions, formal models, and wise informal recommendations about what the government should do and should stop doing to accelerate the rate of recovery from the 2008 financial crisis. The book bristles with ideas, proposals, and rousing discussions. It is hard to put down once you start reading.
—THOMAS J. SARGENT
*William R. Berkley Professor of Economics and Business, New York University, and 2011 Nobel laureate in Economic Sciences*

In contrast to the Washington view that short-term action will right the long-run growth trajectory, the essays here make the case that implementing good long-run policy offers important short-run benefits, too. With the election and 2013 policy debates approaching, *Government Policies and the Delayed Economic Recovery* is a must-read book for policymakers and citizens interested in good policy.
—GLENN HUBBARD
*Dean and Russell L. Carson Professor of Finance and Economics, Graduate School of Business, Columbia University, and former chairman of the Council of Economic Advisers*

Ever since the Great Recession, which began in 2007, the financial crisis, which turned into an outright panic in 2008, and a weak recovery, which started in 2009, the American economy has performed poorly. This book presents the innovative and provocative explanations of highly distinguished and influential thinkers from the Hoover Institution and elsewhere.
—JEREMY BULOW
*Richard Stepp Professor of Economics, Graduate School of Business, Stanford University*

The contributors argue convincingly that by driving up public debt and future taxes, and increasing regulatory costs, policy activism discourages the private commitment of resources needed to grow consumption and investment, create jobs, and advance productivity.
—MARVIN GOODFRIEND
*Professor of economics, Tepper School of Business, Carnegie-Mellon University*

# Government Policies
## and the *DELAYED*
### Economic Recovery

*The Hoover Institution gratefully acknowledges*
*the following individuals and foundations*
*for their significant support of the*
**WORKING GROUP ON ECONOMIC POLICY**

Lynde and Harry Bradley Foundation

John A. Gunn and Cynthia Fry Gunn

Stephen and Sarah Page Herrick

# Government Policies and the *DELAYED* Economic Recovery

*Edited by*

Lee E. Ohanian
John B. Taylor
Ian J. Wright

HOOVER INSTITUTION PRESS

*Stanford University | Stanford, California*

www.hoover.org

Hoover Institution Press Publication No. 627

Hoover Institution at Leland Stanford Junior University,
Stanford, California, 94305-6010

Hoover Institution Press assumes no responsibility for the persistence or accuracy of URLs for external or third-party internet websites referred to in this publication, and does not guarantee that any content on such websites is, or will remain, accurate or appropriate.

First printing 2012
19  18  17  16  15  14  13  12      9  8  7  6  5  4  3  2  1

Manufactured in the United States of America

The paper used in this publication meets the minimum
Requirements of the American National Standard for
Information Sciences—Permanence of Paper for Printed
Library Materials, ANSI/NISO Z39.48-1992. ⊚

Library of Congress Cataloging-in-Publication Data
Government policies and the delayed economic recovery / edited by Lee. E. Ohanian,
John B. Taylor, and Ian J. Wright.
       pages  cm. — (Hoover Institution Press publication ; no. 627)
Includes bibliographical references and index.
ISBN 978-0-8179-1534-6 (cloth) —
ISBN 978-0-8179-1536-0 (e-book)
1. United States—econonmic policy—2009–   2. United States—Economic conditions—2009–
3. Economic development—United States. 4. Ohanian, Lee E., editor of compilation. II. Taylor,
John B., editor of compilation. III. Wright, Ian J., editor of compilation. IV. Series: Hoover
Institution Press publication ; 627.
HC106.84.G68  2012
330.973—dc22                                                                    2012028283

# Contents

# Introduction

## Lee E. Ohanian and John B. Taylor

Economic growth during the recovery from the recession of 2007–09 has been remarkably slow—only 2.4 percent at an annual rate in the first two-and-a-half years. By comparison, economic growth during a comparable period following the deep American recession that ended in 1982 averaged 5.9 percent. Employment growth has also been very weak, with a *smaller* percentage of the working age population now employed than when the recovery began. It is no exaggeration to say that this has been the weakest recovery in American history.

The slow recovery raises a number of important economic and public policy questions. Most important, of course, is what has been the cause of the slow growth? And even if growth eventually picks up, does the long delay signal a new normal of a slow-growth America? Can a slow-growth America lead the world? What can be done to restore robust economic growth in America?

Many economists and policy makers have put forth explanations for the slow growth. For example, Reinhart and Rogoff argue[1] that economic recoveries following financial crises are typically slow, as household debt levels must be reduced and saving rates remain high. While still popular, there are other views. After looking at business cycle experiences throughout American history, Bordo and Haubrich[2] find that recoveries following financial crises are not typically weak. More broadly, a number of countries have recorded very rapid economic growth following severe economic difficulties that significantly impacted their financial systems. This is true of Japan and much of Western Europe following World War II and South Korea following the Korean War. Taken together, data from these countries indicate that understanding the speed of recovery from difficult economic circumstances requires evaluating a broader set of hypotheses.

This book focuses on a completely different explanation for the weak economic growth that the United States is currently experiencing. It explores the possibility that government economic policy itself is the source of the problem. The book centers around six empirical research studies that examine issues from policy uncertainty to increased regulation as the reason for slow growth. The studies are preceded by a "mission statement" from George Shultz which shows how the future of both the American and the world economy is riding on a good diagnosis of the problem and appropriate changes in policy. The papers are followed by a panel with Shultz, Alan Greenspan, and John Cochrane on ways to make the changes. The book concludes with a summary by Ian Wright

1. Reinhart, Carmen M., and Kenneth Rogoff (2009), "The Aftermath of Financial Crises," *American Economic Review* 99(2), 466–472.

2. Bordo, Michael D., and Joseph G. Haubrich (2011), "Deep Recessions, Fast Recoveries, and Financial Crises: Evidence from the American Record," Working Paper on Economic Policy, Hoover Institution.

of the comments at a conference where some of the papers were presented. Taken together, the contributors to this volume offer a broad-based assessment of how government policies are slowing economic growth—by creating uncertainty and unpredictability, by engendering short-term planning horizons, and by depressing the incentives for businesses to hire new workers and invest in capital and new technologies. The contributors also provide a framework for understanding how policies should change to restore strong trend economic growth.

Here is a summary.

## The Importance of Restoring Strong Growth

George Shultz opens the volume by arguing that diagnosing the situation correctly and thus finding a solution to the economic problem of slow growth is extraordinarily important now. If a slow-growth America becomes the new normal for the 21st century, not only will the future prosperity of the United States be sacrificed but so will American leadership worldwide.

Shultz points out that during the last half of the 20th century the world benefited from American economic leadership. One example is the establishment of a multilateral rules-based trading regime after World War II. Another is the American message— bolstered by its visible success—to developing and emerging market economies that reliance on the market system rather than central planning is the key to economic progress.

He argues that since then we have seen the world move closer to markets with hundreds of millions of people escaping poverty. But a slow-growth America will not be able to provide such leadership in the future. And because there is no natural replacement for this leadership, Shultz argues that a restoration of robust economic growth in America is essential for continued prosperity throughout the world.

## Activism and Policy Uncertainty

Following Shultz's opening, Alan Greenspan presents empirical evidence that too much policy activism has been a major factor holding back economic growth in the recent recovery. His analysis focuses on the decline in business investment in long-lived assets—buildings, factories, and large-scale equipment—compared with investment in highly liquid cash and other short-term financial assets. He shows that, after controlling for normal cyclical effects, there is a strong correlation between the decline in such business investment and the recent increase in the deficit. Since these cyclically-adjusted deficits are largely due to more activist fiscal policy, they can thus serve as a metric of activism, providing evidence that the recent increase in activist policy may be the source of the lower business fixed investment and slower growth.

The policy implication of these empirical findings is that a first priority should be to end the short-run temporary stimulus packages and start reducing the deficit immediately. This would reduce the amount of crowding out of investment and start to raise economic growth.

Alan Greenspan also devotes considerable attention to recent economic developments in Europe, arguing that poor economic policy in Greece and other countries that are now in crisis is the likely source of the economic problems currently facing Europe. In particular, he points out that unit labor costs in Greece are well above those in Germany and many other countries in the Eurozone. He shows that wage inflation has been higher in Greece than most of the rest of Europe both before and after Greece joined the Eurozone. But before the euro, currency depreciation (of the old drachma) kept Greece relatively competitive in contrast to what has happened since Greece adopted the euro, which made such depreciation impossible.

Scott Baker, Nick Bloom, and Steve Davis investigate whether policy uncertainty could be a factor causing the recent slow growth. They start by developing a new quantitative index of policy uncertainty, which combines several measures. For example, one of their measures is the number of provisions in the tax code which expire each year. Indeed, this type of temporary tax change is making the entire tax system unpredictable, and thus provides a good measure of policy uncertainty. According to the U.S. Congress's Joint Committee on Taxation, eighty-four tax provisions expired in 2011, about the same number as in 2009 and in 2010. This is ten times greater than the number of provisions that expired in 1999. Other components of the index tell similar though not identical stories. In fact, during the past decade the overall index has increased.

After developing the index and discussing its pros and cons, the authors use time series statistical techniques to test whether changes in the index are correlated with changes in economic growth over time. They find that increases in the index—greater policy uncertainty—tend to be associated with reductions in economic growth. The effect is statistically significant and appears to be timed so that increases in the index lead to reductions in economic growth, suggesting a causal explanation.

## Monetary and Fiscal Policy

Bob Hall examines recent problems with monetary policy. He focuses on the "zero bound" constraint on monetary policy as the reason for the weak economic growth and persistently high unemployment in the recovery. In his model, aggregate demand is weak because monetary policy needs to reduce the interest rate to stimulate investment and especially consumption by the household sector. The constraint is the lower bound of zero on the federal funds rate, which prevents the Fed from lowering the interest rate further. As an example he assumes that the Taylor Rule now calls for an interest rate of −5 percent,[3] which is clearly well below zero.

Hall recommends two policies—"magic bullets," he calls them—which would effectively lower the real interest rate. The first would be to enact a consumption tax that would gradually be phased into the tax law in future years. This would effectively lower the price of current consumption compared with future consumption, and thus stimulate households to consume more now. The second proposal is that the Fed should "stop exchanging reserves for currency at par," in order to break the connection between currency and other assets in the economy.

John Taylor and John Cogan focus on the 2009 fiscal stimulus package, showing that it has not been successful in raising government purchases and thus has been largely ineffective in increasing economic growth. Much of the recent economic debate about the impact of stimulus packages has focused on the size of the government purchases multiplier. But equally crucial is the size of the government purchases multiplicand—the change in government purchases of goods and services that the multiplier actually multiplies.

---

3. The Taylor Rule says that the federal funds rate should equal 1.5 times the inflation rate plus .5 times the GDP gap plus 1. For example, if the inflation rate is 2 percent and the GDP gap is −.5 percent, then the federal funds rate should be 1.5 percent. A federal funds rate reading of −5 percent implies a larger gap, lower inflation, or different coefficients.

Cogan and Taylor find that the American Recovery and Reinvestment Act (ARRA) of 2009 increased federal government purchases as a share of GDP by only .19 percent and infrastructure by only .05 percent at its peak in the third quarter of 2010. While state and local governments received substantial grants under ARRA, they did not use these grants to increase their purchases of goods and services as many had predicted. Instead they reduced borrowing and increased transfer payments. Cogan and Taylor also review research on similar stimulus programs in the 1970s which reveals similar behavior on the part of state and local governments. The paper raises questions about the design and feasibility of such stimulus programs in the federal system of the United States.

## Policy Impacts on Productivity

Ellen McGrattan and Edward Prescott examine the role of adverse productivity shocks due to increased government regulation in the recession and the slow recovery. They start by shedding new light on one of the most puzzling features of the U.S. economy in the recession of 2007–09, as well as in the two previous recessions of 2000–01 and 1991–92. In all three of these recessions, labor productivity, measured as real output per worker hour, did not decline. This behavior of productivity stands in sharp contrast to its pattern in all previous recessions when productivity would move nearly in lockstep with real output. Many economists have interpreted this change in the cyclical pattern of productivity to mean that real business cycle models, which emphasize changes in productivity as an explanation for business cycle fluctuations, are no longer important.

McGrattan and Prescott provide new evidence on the cyclical pattern of productivity, and new support for the importance of productivity in driving cyclical changes in economic activity. They do this by developing a model economy that features intangible capital investment and technological change that is specific to the intangibles sector. Their analysis indicates that standard measures of labor productivity are flawed, because they do not include investment in intangible capital in the measure of real output. McGrattan and Prescott then provide evidence that intangible investment declined in the recent recession and has not yet recovered. Thus, actual productivity is likely to have experienced a negative shock. They then provide data on the increased federal government regulations which suggest that these regulations are a source of the adverse productivity shock.

## Policy Impacts on Labor Markets

Kyle Herkenhoff and Lee Ohanian also address the question of why the recovery has been so weak. They start by documenting that most macroeconomic variables—including real output, consumption, and investment—remain far below trend nearly three years after the recession trough was reached, and that per capita employment today is below its level during the depths of the recession. This weak recovery is particularly puzzling given that corporate profitability and corporate cash positions improved relative to their pre-crisis levels.

They find that an important reason for why employment has not recovered is that various government interventions have depressed labor markets by negatively impacting the incentives for business to hire workers and for workers to accept offers. These interventions include the very expensive programs designed to boost aggregate demand and to support ailing industries, including the

American Recovery and Reinvestment Act, Cash for Clunkers, the home-buyer tax credit, and home mortgage programs, including mortgage modification programs that reduced the incentives for workers to relocate from poor labor markets to better labor markets. By driving up the public debt, these programs also depressed the economy by creating expectations of higher taxes, and also created uncertainty about future taxes as policymakers vacillated over the future course of the Bush tax cuts and the exact nature of tax changes.

To help restore prosperity, Herkenkoff and Ohanian recommend broad-based tax reform that cuts the corporate income tax, equalizes tax treatment across all types of capital, broadens the tax base, confronts entitlement spending, and more broadly reduces government spending, as well as reforming unemployment benefits to reward job acceptance and accumulating human capital.

IN SUM, the contributors to this book consider a wide range of topics and policy issues related to the delayed economic recovery. While their opinions are not always the same, together they reveal a common theme: the delayed recovery has been due to the enactment of poor economic policies and the failure to implement good economic policies. The discussion at the conference where some of the papers were presented—summarized by Ian Wright—reveals a similar theme.

The clear implication is that a change in the direction of economic policy is sorely needed. Simply waiting for economic problems to work themselves out, hoping that growth will improve as the Great Recession of 2007–2009 fades into the distant past, will not be enough to restore strong economic growth in America.

# CHAPTER 1

# Economic Strength and American Leadership

## GEORGE P. SHULTZ[*]

My job, as I see it, is to put into perspective and underline the importance of restoring robust economic growth to America.

Let's start by recollecting the last century. We had wars, including two very large ones with millions of people killed and injured. We had the murderous regimes of Stalin and Hitler and, in a different way, that of Mao. We had social upheaval. We had the Great Depression. We had the ultimate degradation of humanity in the Holocaust. It was an awful century.

At the same time, it's stunning to realize that, since the end of World War II, we have seen probably the greatest burst of human progress ever. We live longer and we're healthier than ever before. To a great extent, that is attributable to the astonishing research that has been done on how the human body works and the iden-

[*] This article is the edited transcript of remarks given at the conference "Restoring Robust Economic Growth in America" at Hoover Institution, Stanford University, on December 2, 2011.

tification of pharmaceuticals, procedures, and devices that have changed the whole outlook on health. To a large degree, those discoveries emanated from work done in the United States.

In the years since the end of World War II, Soviet expansionist tendencies were contained successfully, the Cold War was brought to a satisfactory end with little bloodshed, and an economic and security commons was created on a worldwide basis. Everybody, including the United States, has gained from that commons. Germany and Japan could not have come back so strongly, Europe would not have recovered as successfully, and China and India would not be undergoing their current expansions were it not for the global commons that has been created, largely with leadership from the United States.

Where are we now? Once again, the world is awash in change of a deep, penetrating, seminal nature, and the United States is not leading the way as it once did. Let me briefly identify the nature of the changes that are taking place, why it is essential for our own internal reasons to restore robust economic growth, and why it is essential for the world that the United States stand up and once again show, as Ronald Reagan did, that it is a shining city on a hill.

Consider the changes. The whole face of the world is undergoing drastic change. With the exception of the United States, all developed countries are seeing rates of fertility fall, longevity increase, and labor forces shrink in proportion to their total populations. These changes alter the outlooks and capabilities of countries such as Germany, Italy, Spain, and Portugal. France is holding its own demographically, only because a significant proportion of its population is Muslim, but as this segment of the population is largely unassimilated, it is more of a problem than an asset. Russia has a demographic catastrophe on its hands. Fertility is low and longevity for Russian men is about sixty, which is unbelievable in this day and age, but they're drinking themselves to death. Russian women live twelve years longer than their male counterparts. In some respects, China has the most interesting demography because its fertility rate dropped dramatically beginning about thirty years ago. The result is that for the last quarter-century, China's labor pool has been increasing at a good rate while the number of people the labor pool has to support has been decreasing, so they have had a demographic dividend. That's about to change, almost as if a light switch were being flipped. The labor pool will level off and then start to decrease. I use the term "labor pool" rather than "labor force" because there's so much underemployment in China. Nevertheless, this will be a big change. Furthermore, the number of people the labor force will have to support will be rising rapidly just as the labor pool is falling, so the demographic dividend will disappear and a demographic drag will suddenly take hold.

Looking at Africa, the Middle East, and the Maghreb, a different picture emerges. You see falling but still high fertility, no significant change in longevity, and relatively young populations with all too many young people unemployed. The world is moving toward a drastically different demographic scenario from that of forty years ago.

The United States has a healthy demography but we are jeopardizing it because we are not giving enough of our young people adequate educational opportunities. This is particularly noticeable in California, where there are poor schools in the low-income-per-capita Latino areas with growing populations. This problem needs to be addressed urgently, in my opinion.

In addition, we need to appreciate the depth and the impact of the information and communication revolution that has taken place. Leaders used to have a kind of monopoly on information and the ability to organize and communicate, but that is no longer the case. Almost anybody anywhere can find out practically anything, and they can easily communicate and organize themselves. This is drastically changing the problem of governance. The change is tough on long-standing autocratic regimes, but it's a challenge for open societies as well.

When you combine the information and communication revolution with the demographic situation, particularly in the Maghreb and the Middle East, you have a volatile mix.

It is important to remember that the Arab Spring was set off by the action of a small entrepreneur in Tunisia who wanted to start a small business selling things. His last words were: "All I want to do is work." Remember that phrase, because work attaches people to reality. Without work, there's little sense of reality. The Tunisian shopkeeper wanted to get attached to reality but his government wouldn't allow it.

The third major movement in progress is the Arab Awakening. I don't use the term "spring" because it implies that there is some sort of inevitable progression. At this point, I don't think anybody knows quite where this is going. We must have the ability to work with this seminal development, and it is a powerful reason why we need to restore robust economic growth.

I call what is happening the Arab Awakening, but an awakening is going on all over the world. It is clear enough that China is very concerned about these trends. In an earlier career, I was a labor economist and I served as an arbitrator and mediator. In labor circles, it's said that there is only one thing worse than a wildcat strike, and that's a successful wildcat strike, because success teaches people how to get something to happen. The spreading Arab Awakening is, in a sense, a series of successful wildcat strikes by groups of people who don't know where they're going but know that they have managed to bring down regimes. A seminal change is taking place in an area of the world that is very important in the arenas of energy and religion. If this change spreads to India and Pakistan, which have nuclear weapons, it will potentially create an explosive situation.

We have seen the emergence of random violence, or terrorism, much of it inspired by radical Islam. This phenomenon, particularly noticeable in the last ten years, but which has been going on for quite a long while, has imposed a cost on us that is heavier than many people appreciate. It is more than just taking off your shoes at the airport. Our embassies used to hang out welcome signs; now they look like fortresses. We've had two very costly wars, and there is a general sense of unease, so a heavy cost is being paid.

The state system is no longer what it used to be. We tend to think of the world as being organized into states that interact in certain ways, but the state system, while still key, is eroding. There are many areas, particularly in Africa, where there is little real government. There are other areas that lack a sovereign or orderly government capable of making a difficult deal with another country and having that deal stick. This problem exists even in the ancient nation-states of Europe because, to a degree, they don't know whether they're in a country, a European community, or the Eurozone, so they pass the buck and, in the process, manage to avoid confronting reality. So in many ways the state system is breaking down. The global financial crisis seems to be a toxic combination of governmental and financial incompetence or inability to confront the realities that are facing people and design a strategy to deal with them. I use the term "strategy" because we seem to be capable of implementing only short-term fixes.

When the world was awash in change in the twentieth century, the United States was a global leader that produced ideas, gave crucial support to other countries, and rallied allies. It did not impose its will on others but, to a great extent, it was a shining city on a hill—an example that inspired people around the world. The United States also exerted influence by saying: here is the right course and this is what we're willing to do.

I'll take an example that's totally out of the economic sphere just to make the point. In the 1980s the world was affected by a problem with the ozone layer. We could see that if the ozone layer depleted there would be dire consequences. There were arguments among scientists, but most of them agreed that the ozone layer was being depleted. Even among the doubters, there was no disagreement that total depletion of the ozone layer would be catastrophic, so Ronald Reagan managed to take out an insurance policy called the Montreal Protocol. The United States led in providing the scientific basis for the Protocol. The United States also led in diplomatic efforts to encourage other countries to support the measure. The United States led as an example to the world and the problem was resolved. As it turned out, the scientists who had been alarmed about ozone depletion were right, so action was taken in the nick of time.

U.S. leadership is not as strong now as it was in the 1980s. There are many reasons for this, but certainly a central factor is our economy, which is in the doldrums. People seem to be wondering what can be done. Recently, I read that our secretary of the treasury went to a European meeting and the Austrian finance minister spoke condescendingly to him, basically saying: "What do you know? Don't bother us with your silly advice." Can you imagine the finance minister of Austria saying that to the secretary of the treasury of the United States?

We need to get our house in order and, at least as I see it, there are obvious and simple ways to achieve this goal. At today's meeting, I expect that we will discuss the simple, obvious actions that we should take. We can then transmit them to the powers that be in hopes of getting our country moving forward once again.

# CHAPTER 2

# Uncertainty Unbundled: The Metrics of Activism

ALAN GREENSPAN

My special task is essentially to focus on the short- and intermediate-term issues that relate to the United States. However, these issues can just as readily be expanded to the rest of the developed world, and I will spend some time discussing Europe as well. I agree with George Shultz's opening remarks about American global leadership. It saddens me to say that. It's a terribly gloomy commentary on where we are, coming from someone who has obviously participated in an extraordinarily large amount of public policy for so long.

Beginning with the United States, let me start with the first important question: how is it that we've had such an extraordinarily sluggish, historically unprecedented degree of near stagnation, which in many respects is characteristic of what we saw in the 1930s? (Fortunately not as deep, but the characteristics are the same.) Let me take the current economy and try to define what's wrong with it. Figure 1 shows both nominal and real values of

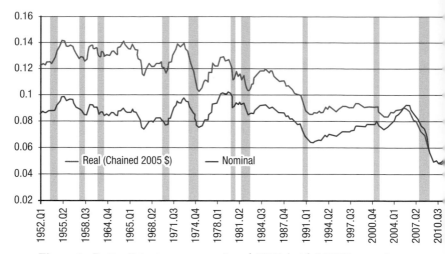

**Figure 1.** Ratio: Private structures / total GDP (with NBER recessions shaded).

*Source:* Greenspan Associates.

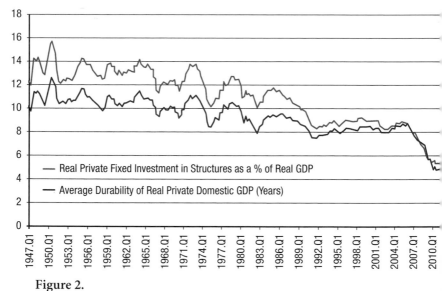

**Figure 2.**

*Source:* Greenspan Associates.

investment in private structures as a share of gross domestic product (GDP).

I present the share both in nominal terms and in real terms just to indicate how significant the differences are. The shaded lines represent National Bureau of Economic Research (NBER) recessions. Note that in every recovery from 1949 forward, a disproportionate amount of the recovery comes from private structures, both residential and non-residential. However, something unprecedented has happened at the tail end of Figure 1: the amount invested in private structures as a percent of GDP steeply declined.

Figure 2 shows my calculation of an average durability of real private domestic GDP, plotted alongside real private fixed investment in structures (as in Figure 1) as a percentage of real GDP.

To obtain the average durability measure, I constructed a vector of all the elements of GDP in its greatest detail and associated each component with a longevity. For example, a haircut is one month. Software is about three-and-a-half years. Residential buildings are seventy-five years. A very large segment of the average age vector is calculated by the Bureau of Economic Analysis as part of its capital stock data system. I used their calculations as much as possible and added my own where necessary. Most services, I assumed, have zero life expectancy. In the end, of course, the longer term components are what drive this calculation. The average durability of private domestic GDP is highly correlated with, and can be proxied by, the investment in private structures.

What would have happened had investment in structures not declined, but rather behaved as it had in the other post-war recoveries? Figure 3 shows that GDP would have replicated the GDP changes of previous recoveries (as shown by the simulated path relative to the actual path of GDP). To compute the simulated

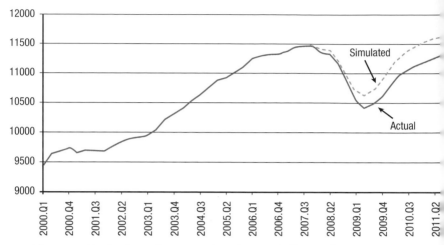

**Figure 3.** Real private domestic GDP (SAAR, billions of 2005 $) through Q3 2011.
*Source:* Greenspan Associates.

path, I assumed that the pre-recession intermediate downward trend in structural investment continued as population growth slowed—you would expect the production of buildings (which are a major part of structures) to be somewhat depressed. Using this hypothetical measure for the structures component of GDP, given that the rest of the GDP followed its actual path to date, produces a reasonable counterfactual GDP forecast.

As shown in Figure 3, there is a fairly significant gap between the actual and the simulated GDP. The cumulative difference between the two represents just over three percentage points of annual GDP, which, by my estimation, is essentially the equivalent of three fewer percentage points in the current unemployment rate. As a consequence, were structures behaving normally, the unemployment rate would be below six percent rather than at about nine percent. And the economy would not be categorized as very sluggish.

In short, we're experiencing a significant reduction of long-lived assets. This results from a very heavy discounting as the time frame moves out from current short-term to longer-term outputs.

Figure 4 shows fixed investment divided by cash flow, for non-farm nonfinancial corporate business, a measure of the share of cash flow that corporate management *chose* to invest. I find this statistic to be one of the most useful means to determine the degree of uncertainty of corporate management, which, of course, has led to heavy discounting and the recent drop-off in investment in structures. Figure 4 shows that management has chosen to invest a very low (almost record low) share of cash flows recently. The ratio is hovering at its lowest levels in the post–World War II period. You have to go back to 1940 to see anything close to it during peacetime.

The numbers suggest that the very long-term outlook is so uncertain that few are investing.

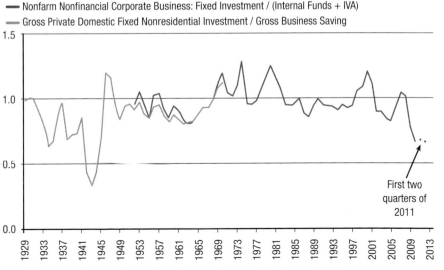

**Figure 4.**  Share of cash flow invested annually through 2010.
*Source:* Greenspan Associates.

Before I joined government, well back into the last century, I worked extensively for corporate management, specifically in the capital investment area. And while that work differs in some ways from today's practices, and differs among companies, two criteria were generally employed to determine what part of the liquid cash flow is appropriate for the company to invest in illiquid long-term assets. We first estimated the expected rate of return (discounted by the corporation's hurdle rate) of a particular facility that the product managers or others within the corporation determined would be useful. If the rate of return of that proposed facility exceeded the cost of capital, then we went to step two. Step two, which turned out to be most important back then as now: the computation of the *variance* of the average forecast. In my experience, what killed most of the prospective capital projects was too large a variance. This is precisely what we are experiencing today.

Short-term capital investment—in equipment and software, for example—as a percent of GDP, is following the path of what we've seen in earlier periods. It's the lack of long-term investment in structures that is creating the problem.

An alternate measure of the extent to which corporations are pulling back is the amount of cash flows remaining in liquid asset investments. Obviously, if a company is not investing, it will end up with either a reduction in debt or some other change on the balance sheet. Most prominently right now, the result has been an increase in liquid assets. Figure 5 illustrates this.

It shows that corporations' holdings of liquid assets have risen sharply over the past two years. That rise does not reflect an affinity for liquid assets, but rather a lack of alternative investment options. A large part of the investment spectrum has been removed from consideration by management owing to long-term uncertainty.

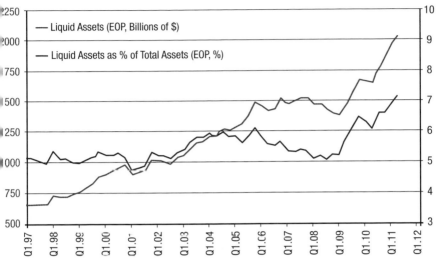

**Figure 5.** U.S. nonfarm nonfinancial corporate business: liquid assets (EOP, billions $) quarterly through Q2 2011.
*Source:* Greenspan Associates.

The share of cash flow that corporations choose to invest in illiquid assets (what I call the "capex" ratio) is a very good operative measure of the degree of uncertainty in the economy. I do not care what management says about uncertainty. I watch how management behaves. The capex ratio measures what corporations *choose* to do. Figure 6 presents my attempt to model this particular measure of uncertainty. It suggests concurrent fiscal policy as a significant source of uncertainty.

I used a linear specification with three independent variables to model the capex ratio. First, I cyclically adjusted the federal deficit as a percent of GDP and include this as an independent variable. This is one of the most interesting and unexpected variables. Its coefficient has an extraordinarily high t-value (–7.75). As I will

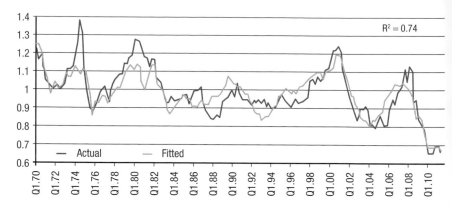

**Figure 6.** Nonfinancial corporate business: fixed investment / cash flow, actual vs. calculated, quarterly 1970 through Q2 2011.

Independent Variable 1: Cyclically Adjusted Federal Deficit / GDP (t−2) [t-value: −7.75].
Independent Variable 2: Nonfarm Operating Rate (t−3) [t-value: 5.89].
Independent Variable 3: Treasury Spread: 30yr–5yr (% p.a.) (t−2) [t-value: −5.92].
Dependent variable specified in log form.
Deficit variable specified as in [1+(Cyc Adj Deficit / GDP)].
t-statistics calculated using Newey-West HAC standard errors and covariance.
*Source:* Greenspan Associates.

note later, it suggests a very large amount of concurrent crowding out of private capital investment as a consequence of the deficit itself. Flow-of-Funds data make it very clear that this is happening *ex post.*

The nonfarm operating rate with a significant lag (three quarters) and a t-value of 5.89 accounts for an important amount of loss of capital investment because the nonfarm operating rate is a reasonably good proxy for corporate profitability. Its effect, of course, is not a function of government policies except indirectly in that government activism, overall, has reduced the level of GDP. The reason I find a significant lag for the nonfarm operating rate is that capital expenditures, shown in the chart as part of the capex ratio, are actually spent well after the decision to invest is made, positioning capital expenditures as a lagging variable. The concurrent variables are capital appropriations or new orders. Thus, if I had capital appropriations data I would use them, but unfortunately they are no longer collected.

Lastly, Figure 7 shows the spread between the 30-year and 10-year notes, and the spread between the 10-year and 5-year notes, the combination of which comprises the third independent variable.

Both spreads show very much the same thing: an extraordinary rise in the slope of what we would call the term structure. The correlation between the two spreads implies a steady rise and fall of the 25-year spread. The 25-year spread is the largest I can find going back to *before* the Great Depression.

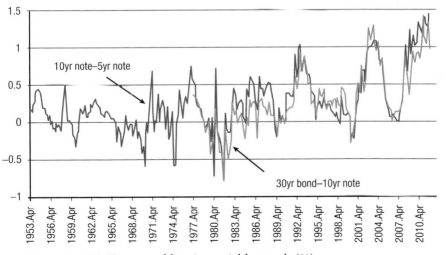

**Figure 7.** U.S. Treasury obligations: yield spreads (%).
*Source:* Greenspan Associates.

What I find fascinating is that we have never seen as much aversion to very long-term investments as there is today. This tells us a great deal, not only about the level of uncertainty but about the nature of the uncertainty. As Figure 6 shows, the t-stat on the coefficient estimate of the treasury spread variable (30-year minus 5-year) has a magnitude near 6.

To understand the reason why we're getting such an extraordinary, immediate impact of the deficit in Figure 6, I turn to Figure 8, which plots gross saving minus fixed investment (*ex post*).

Most of the modeling on the relationship of the deficit and interest rates had been done previously by regressing long-term interest rates against the Congressional Budget Office's (CBO) long-term projections. But what is more fascinating to me is the short-term, contemporaneous data, which are essentially a measure of crowding out. In Figure 8 one can see the difference from 2006 to 2011

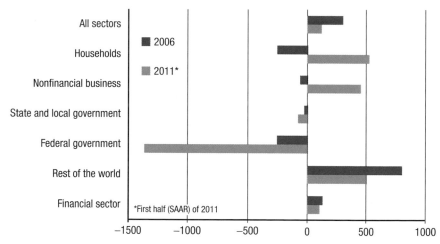

**Figure 8.** Gross saving less fixed investment (billions of $).
*Source:* Greenspan Associates.

directly. By definition, savings less fixed investment should equal inventory change and data discrepancy. This is represented by the top category in the figure, "All sectors" consolidated. The increase in the federal government's deficit from 2006 to 2011 relative to other sectors tells us that the huge government deficit has snuffed out investment in two major segments of the economy: nonfinancial business and households. It is crowding out those borrowers with very poor credit ratings (CCC, for example).

I haven't said anything about residential construction because it's behaving very much the same way that nonresidential construction is behaving, and for much the same reasons. The major collapse in homebuilding occurred statistically as a consequence of a dramatic shift in the proportion of total occupied housing units that are owner-occupied. Owner-occupied units were rising at a rate of over a million a year during the early part of last decade, creating a very large increase in starts of single-family homes. But as the propensity to go into owner occupancy began to fade from 2005 forward as home price increases slowed, there was a dramatic drop in single-family home construction. A major part of that propensity to move away from homeownership and into renting is a reflection of the elimination of a very significant factor in home purchase choice—the expectation of rising prices. This is very similar to the change that has taken place in corporations: refraining from fixed investment and instead choosing to invest their cash flows in liquid assets. In the household sector, the same effect appears as households move out of long-term assets, including homes and consumer durable goods. The ratio of household savings to fixed investment appears very similar to what we're seeing in the corporate sector. Both reflect an expectation of diminished profitability over the long run.

As shown in Figure 6, seventy-four percent of the variation in the capex ratio (and so uncertainty) is explained by the three variables I include. The major issue, which I've not been able to fully explain, is where the rest of the variation is coming from, as twenty-six percent is a large residual to be explained. The reason is that uncertainty is very difficult to model. Undoubtedly, a small part of the effect on uncertainty is the residual effect of the crisis itself. But my regression is a forty-year regression, and the extent to which the crisis matters can't be very large on coefficient estimates. Another part of the effect undoubtedly exists because of the Dodd-Frank Act. As a corporate manager, the inability to know whether you're going to be able to get financing is an element that factors into the variance of the expected rates of return on long-term assets.

The basic notion that what we need is more stimulus (uncertainty-creating activism) is badly misplaced. The stimulus program (which is now distributed quarterly by the Bureau of Economic Analysis), from the first quarter of 2009 forward, regresses well against the capex ratio. In other words, we are displacing a very large amount of private investment with the aggregate stimulus. And I'm increasingly persuaded that the remaining unexplained variation has to do with other elements of politically driven uncertainty. I am not arguing against the impact multipliers that are being employed by the CBO in order to judge the effect of the stimulus, but I am saying they are missing offsets that are potentially large. The impact multipliers are gross, but what we need is net, assuming it is still positive, which is yet another unknown.

Having said that, I focus on the impact multipliers because they come from our standard econometric models, none of which captured the most important economic event of the last eight decades:

the recent financial crisis. The list includes the models of the Federal Reserve, the IMF, and J. P. Morgan, among many others. Why we assume that using the coefficients of models that don't work is going to give us a reasonable estimate of the stimulus impact of a particular government program is puzzling to me. I am very disturbed by the general consensus of the profession that these multipliers are being measured correctly. I have my doubts.

## Europe

There is no way to have any sense of the outlook for the United States if we don't factor in the effects coming from Europe.

Figure 9 plots unit labor costs in early 2011 of the major euro countries against their 10-year sovereign spreads in 2011, all relative to Germany.

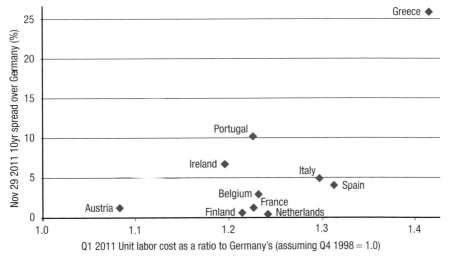

**Figure 9.** Unit labor cost vs. 10-year bond spread ($\rho = 0.70$).

*Source:* Greenspan Associates.

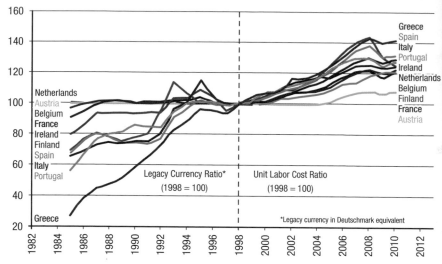

**Figure 10.** Unit labor costs as a ratio to Germany's (1998 = 100).
*Source:* Greenspan Associates.

One can see a strong correlation and, as expected, Greece is at the top, with the prudent Austria at the bottom. The correlation coefficient is an indication that falling competitiveness of the individual economies is showing up in the extent to which their spreads rise relative to Germany.

Figure 10 plots unit labor costs over time relative to those of Germany.

Figure 10 shows that, prior to the onset of the euro, competitiveness was maintained by serial devaluations. (I'm exhibiting countries in terms of deutschmarks as a proxy for the euro prior to its onset.) Many countries did not need to make a significant change from their earlier periods when entering the Eurozone. Greece certainly did. The unit labor costs of Greece, first in deutschmarks and then in euros, form a steep, nearly straight line throughout the sample. Nothing apparently changed in the behavior of Greece when it adopted the euro. I proxy culture by a country's savings rate, its degree of inflation (prudence), and adherence to the rule of law proxied by the size of its shadow economy.

In Figure 11 I exhibit relative savings rates, in this case including the United States for comparison. The rankings are largely the same.

Figure 12, the GDP (value added) deflator as a ratio to Germany's, exhibits much the same pattern shown for unit labor costs.

We can similarly examine measures of the state of the shadow economy in Europe. Figure 13 measures the amount of tax evasion and illegal commerce as a percent of GDP in European countries. Again, similar rankings.

Euro-south members, no longer having the safety valve of devaluation to maintain competitiveness, are forced to run cur-

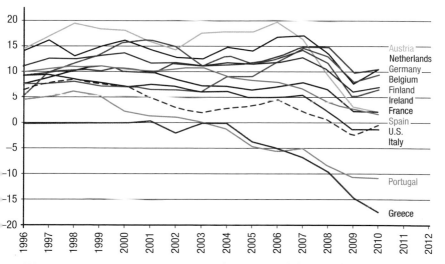

**Figure 11.** Net savings as a percent of net national disposable income.
*Source:* Greenspan Associates.

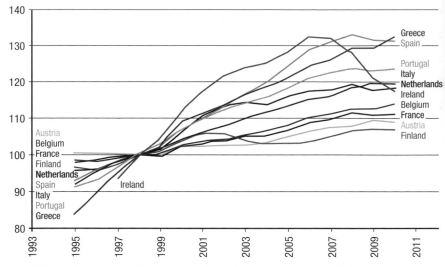

**Figure 12.** GDP deflator as a ratio to Germany's (1998 = 100).

*Source:* Greenspan Associates.

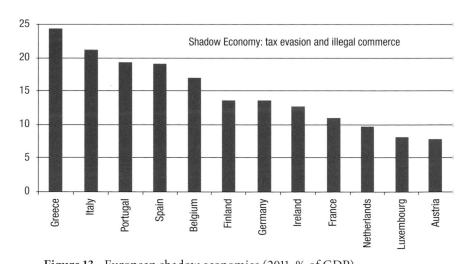

**Figure 13.** European shadow economies (2011, % of GDP).

*Source:* Friedrich Schneider, PhD, Chair of the Department of Economics, Johannes Kepler University, Linz, Austria.

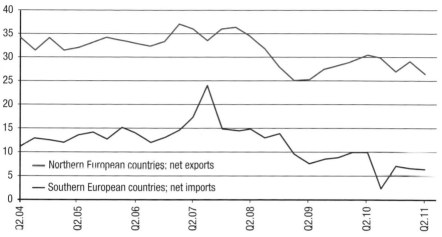

**Figure 14.** Net exports and imports of goods and services intra-Eurozone 16 (SA, billions of €).

*Source:* Greenspan Associates.

rent account deficits financed by their Euro-north neighbors (Figure 14).

In Figure 15, for the year 2010 I show federal government deficits as a percent of GDP, matched against unit labor cost as a ratio to that of Germany for the first quarter of 2011. No surprises. Again we find very similar results to the previous figures.

Figure 16 shows that there has been a huge increase in consumption in the southern Eurozone countries relative to Germany over the past decade and a half.

In short, the transfers depicted by net exports and imports in Figure 14 are real transfers. And not only transfers, but transfers that are being consumed. The southern countries didn't save the transfers; they consumed them.

Figures 17 and 18 show the 10-year sovereign yield spreads over Germany since December of 1991. I suspect the reason the euro

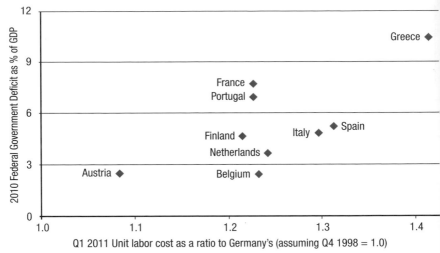

**Figure 15.** Unit labor cost vs. federal deficit (% of GDP) (ρ = 0.69).

*Note:* Ireland excluded.

*Source:* Greenspan Associates.

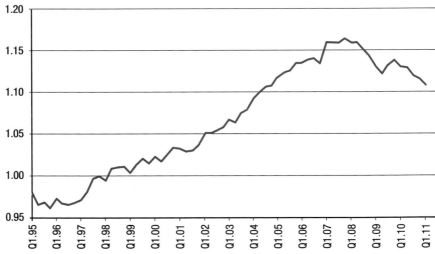

**Figure 16.** Southern Eurozone countries (Greece, Italy, Portugal, and Spain): real final consumption as a ratio to Germany's.

*Source:* Greenspan Associates.

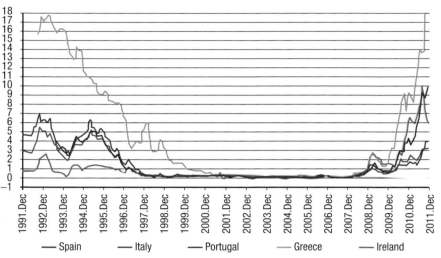

**Figure 17.** 10-year sovereign note yield spread over the German Bund (monthly average, %).

*Source:* Greenspan Associates.

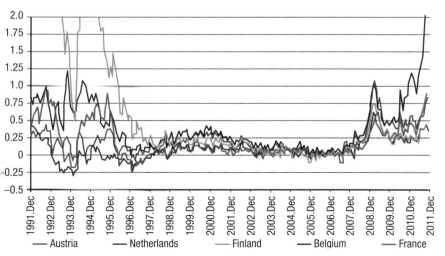

**Figure 18.** 10-year sovereign note yield spread over the German Bund (monthly average, %).

*Source:* Greenspan Associates.

lasted as long as it did, given the cultural inconsistencies, was a global boom that enabled everyone to be financed.

It is quite extraordinary to see these countries, after almost a decade of narrow interest rate spreads against the Bund, blow out again. But the system had to break down eventually and it's happening now. The countries that were the culturally least prudent before the euro are turning out to create the biggest problems today. In short, there is no evidence of cultural change.

I myself sat in on some of the discussions that occurred prior to the onset of the euro even though I was not, obviously, involved in any decision making. There was a firm belief and general expectation—in the markets, for example—that Italians, once in the Eurozone, were going to behave like Germans. They didn't. Neither did the Greeks, the Spaniards, or the Portuguese. The question is, can you have a single currency with multiple diverse cultures? The answer, based on the experiment we've just been through, is that you cannot. As a result the Eurozone is moving rapidly towards fiscal consolidation. Yet that outcome seems itself unstable since it's inconceivable to me (just to add to the level of pessimism) that sovereign nations are going to allow their budgets to be determined by Germany, which seems ultimately to be the case.

# CHAPTER 3

# Has Economic Policy Uncertainty Hampered the Recovery?

Scott R. Baker, Nicholas Bloom, and Steven J. Davis[*]

## Introduction

The U.S. economy hit bottom in June 2009. Thirty months later, output growth remains sluggish and unemployment still hovers above 8 percent. A critical question is why. One view attributes the weak recovery, at least in part, to high levels of uncertainty about economic policy. This view entails two claims: First, that economic policy uncertainty has been unusually high in recent years. Second, that high levels of economic policy uncertainty caused households and businesses to hold back significantly on spending, investment, and hiring. We take a look at both claims in this article.

We start by considering an index of economic policy uncertainty developed in Baker, Bloom, and Davis (2012). Figure 1, which plots our index, indicates that economic policy uncertainty fluctuates strongly over time. The index shows historically high

[*] We acknowledge research support from National Science Foundation, the Initiative on Global Markets at the University of Chicago Booth School of Business, and the Stigler Center for the Study of the Economy and the State at the University of Chicago.

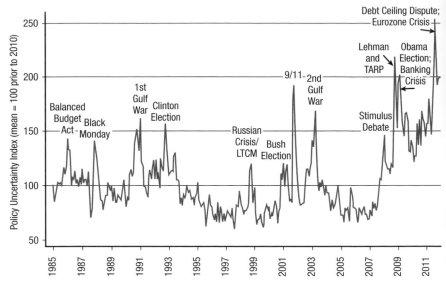

**Figure 1.**  Index of economic policy uncertainty, January 1985 to December 2011.

*Notes:* The index is an aggregation of four components: a scaled count of news articles that refer to the economy, uncertainty, and policy; a time-discounted sum of scheduled expirations of federal tax code provisions; and indexes of disagreement among professional forecasters about future CPI levels and about government purchases of goods and services. See text for details. Data and updates are available at www.policy uncertainty.com.

levels of economic policy uncertainty in the last four years. It reached an all-time peak in August 2011.

As discussed below, we also find evidence that policy concerns account for an unusually high share of overall economic uncertainty in recent years. Moreover, short-term movements in overall economic uncertainty more closely track movements in policy-related uncertainty in the past decade than in earlier periods.

In short, our analysis provides considerable support for the first claim of the policy uncertainty view.

The second claim is harder to assess because it raises the difficult issue of identifying a causal relationship. We do not provide a definitive analysis of the second claim. We find evidence that increases in economic policy uncertainty foreshadow declines in output, employment, and investment. While we cannot say that economic policy uncertainty necessarily causes these negative developments—since many factors move together in the economy—we can say with some confidence that high levels of policy uncertainty are associated with weaker growth prospects.

## Economic Policy Uncertainty over Time

Figure 1 plots our monthly index of economic policy uncertainty from January 1985 to December 2011. (Regular updates are available at www.policyuncertainty.com.) Before describing the construction of the index, we briefly consider its evolution over time.

The policy uncertainty index shows pronounced spikes associated with the Balanced Budget Act of 1985, other major policy developments, the Gulf Wars, the 9/11 terrorist attack, financial scares and crises, and consequential national elections. Policy uncertainty shoots upward around these events, and typically falls back down within a few months. The experience since January 2008 is distinctive, however, in that policy uncertainty rose sharply and stayed at high levels. The last two years are especially noteworthy in this respect. While the most threatening aspects of the financial crisis were contained by the middle of 2009, the policy uncertainty index stood at high levels throughout 2010 and 2011.

The index shows a sharp spike in January 2008, which saw two large, surprise interest rate cuts. The Economic Stimulus Act of 2008, signed into law on 13 February 2008, was also a major focus of economic policy concerns in January 2008. The policy uncertainty index jumps to yet higher levels with the collapse of Lehman Brothers on 15 September 2008 and the enactment in early October of the Emergency Economic Stabilization Act, which created the Troubled Asset Relief Program (TARP). A series of later developments and policy fights—including the debt-ceiling dispute between Republicans and Democrats in the summer of 2011, and ongoing banking and sovereign debt crises in the Eurozone area— kept economic policy uncertainty at very high levels throughout 2011.

## Constructing Our Index of Economic Policy Uncertainty

So how do we construct our index? We build several index components and then aggregate over the components to obtain the index displayed in Figure 1. We briefly describe each index component and the aggregation method here. Interested readers can consult Baker, Bloom, and Davis (2012, hereafter BBD) for more details.

### News-Based Component

Our first index component quantifies newspaper coverage of policy-related economic uncertainty. Basically, we measure the monthly frequency of newspaper articles that contain terms related to the economy, uncertainty, and policy. The idea is that a greater number of news articles about economic policy uncertainty reflects the fact that households and businesses are facing a higher level of economic policy uncertainty. This news-based proxy for the level of policy uncertainty is by no means perfect, but we think it provides a useful indicator.

How exactly do we proceed? We consider ten newspapers: the *Wall Street Journal,* the *New York Times,* the *Washington Post, USA Today,* the *Chicago Tribune,* the *Boston Globe,* the *San Francisco Chronicle,* the *Los Angeles Times,* the *Miami Herald,* and the *Dallas Morning News.* We conduct an automated search of all articles in each newspaper from January 1985 to December 2011. For each newspaper, we obtain a count for the number or articles that contain three sets of terms. The first set is {economy, economic}, the second is {uncertain, uncertainty}, and the third is {policy, regulation, Federal Reserve, tax, spending, budget, deficit}. To make it into our count, an article must contain at least one word from all three sets. These search criteria would, for example, flag an article from the *New York Times* that contains the words "economic," "uncertainty," and "tax."

Of course, the raw count of articles that satisfy our search criteria might be influenced by changes over time in the length or total number of articles. So, rather than use the raw monthly count of articles that meet the search criteria, we scale by the number of articles in the same paper containing the word "today." Finally, we combine the scaled count for the ten individual newspapers to form our monthly news-based index of economic policy uncertainty.[1]

---

1. Specifically, we first scale each paper's raw monthly count by a one-sided thirty-six-month moving average of the "today" count in the same paper. We then normalize the scaled counts so that the time-series standard deviation is the same for all newspapers. Next, we sum the normalized scaled counts across newspapers by month to obtain our news-based index of economic policy uncertainty. As a final normaliza-

As a robustness check, we applied the same approach to a news-based index of economic policy uncertainty using Google News, which covers hundreds of newspapers and online news sources. The correlation between our Google News index of economic policy uncertainty and our ten-paper index is 0.76 in the monthly data. We use the 10-paper index as a component of our overall index, because the underlying sources for Google News vary over time in ways that we cannot directly observe or control. Nevertheless, the broader coverage of Google News is quite useful for some purposes, and our work in BBD exploits both the ten-paper approach and the Google News approach.

We also conducted several cross-checks to evaluate the news-based approach. One check uses the news-based approach to construct an index of uncertainty about stock prices. Specifically, as discussed in BBD, we use automated searches to obtain a (scaled) count for the number of news articles with at least one term from all three of the following sets: {economy, economic}, {uncertain, uncertainty}, and {"stock market," "stock price," "equity price"}. We compare this news-based index of stock market uncertainty to the VIX—the Chicago Board of Options Exchange Index of implied volatility in the S&P 500 stock price index. The two indexes move closely together. That is, our news-based index of stock market uncertainty closely mirrors the leading index of stock market uncertainty based on asset prices. The success of the news-based approach at tracking movements in uncertainty about stock prices gives us confidence that the same approach can accurately track other aspects of economic uncertainty.

tion, we divide the news-based index by its mean from January 1985 to December 2009 and multiply the result by 100.

## Scheduled Tax-Code Expirations

A second component of our overall index exploits data on federal tax code provisions that, as a matter of current law, are scheduled to expire at specified future dates. Many of these provisions are "temporary" tax measures that may or may not be extended, with Congress often waiting until the last minute and engaging in large political fights over them. These political debates cause uncertainty for the households and businesses affected by the provisions.

A recent example involves the federal government's use of temporary payroll tax cuts. The Tax Relief, Unemployment Insurance Reauthorization, and Job Creation Act of 2010 instituted a temporary cut in the payroll tax rate, with expiration scheduled for 31 December 2011. The sluggish nature of the recovery in 2011 prompted many calls to extend the payroll tax cut for a second year. The possibility of an extension, and how to cover the revenue loss, became an increasingly contentious and partisan political issue as the expiration date drew nearer. After much back and forth, Congress finally approved an extension on 23 December 2011—but only for two months. Then, just days before the tax cut's expiration in late February, it was extended until the end of 2012, allowing Congress to wait until after the November 2012 elections to decide the fate of the policy.[2] This type of legislative indecision and last-minute action undermines the stability of and certainty about the tax code.

To quantify the frequency and importance of scheduled tax code expirations, we rely on data from the Congressional Budget

---

2. CBO (2012) contains some discussion of recent payroll tax cut provisions and their budgetary consequences.

Office (CBO). Since 1991, the CBO produces annual reports that list federal tax code provisions set to expire over the next ten years. Using these data, we construct a discounted sum of future tax code expirations. This discounted sum serves as the tax code expiration component of our overall economic policy uncertainty index.

This index component shows rapid growth over the past decade in the discounted volume of scheduled tax code expirations. By 2011, the volume of tax code provisions set to expire is about five times larger than in the late nineties. BBD also construct another index of scheduled tax code provisions, using data from the Joint Congressional Committee on Taxation (JCT), and obtain very similar results. The CBO, and presumably the JCT, did not produce data on scheduled tax code expirations before 1991 because the volume was too small to matter. In short, the evidence on scheduled tax code expirations indicates that the federal tax system has become an increasingly important source of uncertainty for businesses and households.

## Forecaster Disagreement about Inflation and Government Purchases

For the third set of components in our policy uncertainty index, we consider disagreement amongst economic forecasters. We use data from the Federal Reserve Bank of Philadelphia, which surveys about fifty professional forecasters every quarter. We look at how much the forecasters disagree on, firstly, the Consumer Price Index measure of quarterly inflation four quarters ahead and, secondly, on the level of government purchases of goods and services four quarters ahead. Larger forecast differences presumably indicate larger differences of opinion, which suggests more uncertainty about future developments than if forecasters mostly agree. Conversely, we take smaller forecast differences to indicate less uncertainty.

To measure disagreement about future inflation, we compute the interquartile range—the spread between the 75th and 25th percentiles—of the four-quarter-ahead forecasts for the quarterly inflation rate. For government purchases, we follow the survey and treat federal government purchases separately from state and local purchases. That is, we compute an interquartile spread measure for the four-quarter-ahead forecasts of federal government purchases, and we compute an analogous measure for state and local government purchases. We then sum the two measures, weighting by size of purchases, to obtain our index component for uncertainty about future government purchases of goods and services.[3]

The disagreement indexes point to relatively high levels of uncertainty about future inflation in the first six years of our sample period (i.e., from 1985 to 1991), during 2008 and early 2009, and again since late 2010. They also show a pattern of high and volatile uncertainty about future government purchases in the first eight years of our sample period and again since the fourth quarter of 2008. The recent increase in uncertainty about

---

3. Specifically, we compute the interquartile range of four-quarter-ahead fore-casts of federal government purchases of goods and services, scaled by the median four-quarter ahead forecast of the same quantity. We then multiply by a five-year backward-looking moving average for the ratio of nominal federal purchases to nominal GDP. These steps yield a sub-index of forecaster disagreement about federal government purchases. After obtaining an analogous sub-index of disagreement for state and local purchases, we sum the two sub-indexes, weighting by the relative size of their purchases.

government purchases is more pronounced at the state and local level than the federal level.

## Aggregating the Components to Obtain an Index of Economic Policy Uncertainty

To aggregate the components into our overall index of economic policy uncertainty, we give 50 percent weight to the news-based component, as it is the broadest measure, and equal weights to the scheduled tax code expiration component, the inflation disagreement component, and the government purchases disagreement component. All components show an increase in economic policy uncertainty in recent years, although to varying degrees. Because the index components share many similarities, the behavior of the overall index is not very sensitive to different weighting schemes, as we show in BBD.

## Policy Uncertainty and Overall Economic Uncertainty

A useful feature of the news-based approach to measuring uncertainty is its flexibility. We exploit that flexibility to quantify the extent to which policy-related uncertainty accounts for overall economic uncertainty. We also use the news-based approach to uncover specific sources of policy uncertainty. For these exercises, we rely on data from Google News. The higher volume of news articles captured by Google News is especially useful when we slice the data into particular policy categories.

Figure 2 shows two indexes. The lower data line is our Google News-based index of economic policy uncertainty, constructed using the method we described above for the ten-paper index.

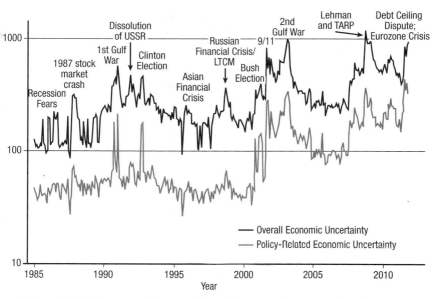

**Figure 2.** Policy uncertainty and overall economic uncertainty, January 1985 to December 2011.

*Note:* The index of overall economic uncertainty is a scaled count of Google News articles that refer to the economy and uncertainty. The index of policy-related uncertainty is a scaled count of Google News articles that refer to the economy, uncertainty, and policy. See text for details.

The upper line is an analogous count of articles that mention the economy and uncertainty but may or may not mention policy. So, if a news article talks about the economy, uncertainty and policy, it shows up in both indexes. If it talks about the economy and uncertainty but does not mention policy, it shows up only in the index given by the upper line.

Comparing the two lines, we see that many articles from 1985 to 2000 mention economic uncertainty but don't refer to policy. That's the gap between the upper and the lower lines. Certain episodes, recession fears in the second half of the 1980s, for example, generated a lot of talk about economic uncertainty but not much talk about policy.

Since 9/11, however, and especially from 2008 onwards, the two lines move together closely, and the gap between the lines is smaller (especially in proportional terms). So when news articles talk about economic uncertainty in recent years, they typically also discuss policy. Moreover, BBD show that the news-based index of economic uncertainty is more highly correlated with the news-based index of policy uncertainty in recent years than in the period before 9/11. These results support the view that policy-related concerns have become a more important source of economic uncertainty.

The obvious next question is: which aspects of policy are the most important sources of economic uncertainty? In BBD, we drill into the details of the articles in Google News that meet our criteria for economic policy uncertainty. We use more refined search criteria to construct counts for twelve broad categories of economic policy such as monetary policy, taxes, health care, financial market regulation, labor market regulation, and so on.

Here is a summary of what we find:

1. Monetary policy accounts for about one-third of policy-related economic uncertainty in the period from 1985 to 2011. Concerns related to taxes, government spending, and fiscal policy appear even more important, accounting for about 40 percent.
2. The historically high levels of economic policy uncertainty in 2010 and 2011 predominantly reflect concerns about taxes and monetary policy. Policy uncertainty in these two areas is more than four

times higher in the last two years than on average from 1985 to 2011, judging by frequency counts of news articles.

3. Although much less pronounced, we also find elevated levels of policy uncertainty in 2010 and 2011 in several other categories: entitlement programs, health care, financial regulation, labor regulation, and sovereign debt and currency issues.

In short, our analysis indicates that the historically high levels of policy uncertainty in 2010 and 2011 mainly reflect concerns about tax and monetary policy and secondarily a broader range of other policy-related concerns.

In BBD, we also approach the connection between economic uncertainty and policy in a different way by examining the sources of stock market volatility. We first identify all daily movements in the U.S. stock market by more than 2.5 percent, up or down, from 1980 to 2011. We then consult the next day's *New York Times*, which invariably contains a major article about the big move. Usually, the article offers a broad explanation for the move in the first paragraph. We review these articles and, on that basis, allocate each big stock-market move into one of several categories such as news about corporate earnings, macroeconomic news, policy-related news, and so on.

Not surprisingly, we find a dramatic increase in the frequency of big daily stock market moves in the 2008–2011 period relative to the previous 28 years. More interestingly for present purposes, the number of big moves attributed to policy news skyrocketed from about one per year in the 1980–2007 period to twelve events per year from 2008 to 2011. The share of big moves attributed to policy rose to 39 percent in the past four years compared to 14 percent of a much smaller number in the earlier period. We see this evidence as strongly confirming the claim that policy uncertainty has been extraordinarily high in the past four years. Insofar as equity market volatility is harmful to the economy, this evidence also lends support to that claim that policy uncertainty has been a factor slowing the recovery.

## Does Economic Policy Uncertainty Matter for the Economy?

Given the evidence pointing to high policy uncertainty in recent years, it is natural to ask how much policy uncertainty matters for economic performance. At this point in our analysis, we must recognize that identifying causal relationships in macroeconomic data is very hard. What we can do is talk a bit about the theoretical connections between uncertainty and economic performance. We can also investigate empirically whether high levels of economic policy uncertainty are associated with weaker growth prospects.

In the theoretical realm, the economics literature has focused on three channels. The first is the real options effect. There is a long literature on this topic and, in fact, one of the best known and earliest pieces is a paper by Ben Bernanke (1983) titled "Irreversibility, Uncertainty and Business Cycles," recently extended and quantified by Bloom (2009) and Bloom et al. (2012). The premise is that when firms are uncertain, it is expensive to invest or disinvest and to hire or fire. So uncertainty encourages firms to delay, more so for longer-lived investments and decisions that are costlier to reverse. The second channel is similar but works on the consumption side. Households become more likely to postpone spending when uncertainty is high, particularly on consumer durables like cars and major appliances—something Romer (1990) regards as a key driver of the drop in demand during the Great Depression. So high uncertainty encourages people to spend less and to build up a buffer stock of liquid assets.

A third channel involves financing costs. Higher uncertainty can raise the cost of capital, especially because much of policy uncertainty is macroeconomic in character and thus hard to diversify. Moreover, because many managers are not diversified in their wealth holdings—they often have explicit or implicit equity stakes in their employers—higher uncertainty encourages managers to adopt a cautious stance toward risk taking and investment (Panousi and Papanikolaou, 2011). As these brief remarks suggest, economic theory identifies reasons to suspect that high levels of policy uncertainty might undermine economic performance.

To approach the issue empirically, in BBD we estimate vector autoregressions (VARs) that include measures of output, employment, prices, stock market levels, and interest rates. We regress current levels of these variables on their lagged values and look at what predicts what. Figure 3 summarizes one of our main results in the form of estimated dynamic relationships. The top graph displays the estimated path of industrial production following a shock to the policy uncertainty measure from Figure 1. Similarly, the bottom graph displays the estimated path for employment.

These graphs are predictions, based on an underlying statistical model, of what would happen over the subsequent three years if policy uncertainty increases by the amount of the actual change from 2006 to 2011. Because the underlying statistical model is linear, we can turn the graphs upside down to get the predicted increase in output and employment if current levels of policy uncertainty returned to 2006 levels. To be clear, we cannot say that

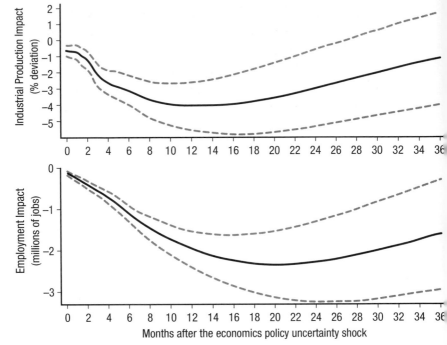

**Figure 3.** Industrial production and employment responses to an increase in economic policy uncertainty.

*Notes:* Impulse response functions for industrial production and employment to a 112-unit increase in the policy-related uncertainty index (the measured increase from 2006 to 2011). Estimated using a monthly vector autoregression on data from 1985 to 2011.

the dynamic relationships displayed in Figure 3 are causal without invoking strong assumptions. But we can say that a return to 2006 levels of policy uncertainty, similar to the average level over our sample period, would appear to be good news for future employment and output growth.

Pastor and Veronesi (2011) identify another potential negative aspect of policy uncertainty. They use our index to show that firm-level equity returns move together more closely when policy uncertainty is high, especially in the period since 2000. Greater co-movement in firm-level stock returns makes it harder for investors to diversify financial risks. That leaves investors with greater risk exposures and is likely to discourage risk taking, as discussed above. High levels of policy uncertainty probably lead to stronger co-movement of firm-level equity returns because much of the policy-related uncertainty is macroeconomic in nature.

## Concluding Remarks

This article summarizes our efforts to measure economic policy uncertainty and assess its effects on economic performance. Our research is ongoing, but we draw a few preliminary conclusions at this point:

- Policy uncertainty has been at historically high levels over the past four years. This conclusion finds support in our new index of economic policy uncertainty and in our analysis of the factors that precipitate big movements in the stock market.
- Policy-related concerns now account for a large share of overall economic uncertainty. Here as well, this conclusion finds support in both the analysis of our news-based indexes and in our investigation into the factors that precipitate big stock market moves.
- A rise in policy uncertainty, similar in magnitude to the actual change since 2006, is associated with substantially lower levels of output and employment over the subsequent thirty-six months.

We think the weight of the evidence and the lessons of economic theory argue for assigning some weight to the policy uncertainty

view. If policymakers can deliver a policy environment character-
ized by greater certainty and stability, there will likely be a positive
payoff in the form of improved macroeconomic performance.

## References

Baker, Scott, Nicholas Bloom, and Steven J. Davis (2012), "Measuring Economic Policy Uncertainty," University of Chicago and Stanford University.
Available at www.policyuncertainty.com.

Bernanke, Ben (1983), "Irreversibility, Uncertainty and Cyclical Investment,"
*Quarterly Journal of Economics* 98, 85–106.

Bloom, Nicholas (2009), "The Impact of Uncertainty Shocks," *Econometrica,*
77, 623–685.

Bloom, Nicholas, Max Floetotto, Nir Jaimovich, Itay Saporta-Ecksten, and
Stephen Terry (2012), "Really Uncertain Business Cycles," Stanford
mimeo. Available at http://www.stanford.edu/~nbloom/RUBC.pdf.

Congressional Budget Office, Congress of the United States (2012), "The Budget and Economic Outlook: Fiscal Years 2012 to 2022." Available at www
.cbo.gov/ftpdocs/126xx/doc12699/01-31-2012_Outlook.pdf.

Pastor, Lubos and Pietro Veronesi (2011), "Political Uncertainty and Risk Pre-
mia," University of Chicago Working Paper.

Panousi, Vasia and Dimitris Papanikolaou (2011), "Investment, Idiosyncratic
Risk and Ownership," forthcoming *Journal of Finance.*

Romer, Christina (1990), "The Great Crash and the Onset of the Great
Depression," *Quarterly Journal of Economics,* 105, 597–624.

# CHAPTER 4

# How the Financial Crisis Caused Persistent Unemployment

ROBERT E. HALL

My topics are the current state of the economy, how we got here, why the recession is lasting so long, and why it will probably last well into the future. At the end, I will describe two blue-sky policies that could end the situation virtually overnight.

In my reading, the primary source of the current state of the economy is simple—it's that people aren't buying enough stuff. In other words, there was a large adverse shift in product demand. That resulted from forces leading up to the financial crisis, some direct effects of the crisis itself on financial institutions, and the resulting de-leveraging of the household. My reading of the data is that the central problem on the expenditure side of the economy arises within the household. Household consumption comprises two-thirds of GDP, so it's not surprising that it should play a large role. The non-household part of private expenditure—that's plant and equipment investment—seems to have actually outperformed its normal response to a collapse of consumption. The source of low output and employment in today's economy is the huge decline in household spending.

## 1. Taylor Rules

Prior to the crisis, the United States, along with other advanced economies, had come to rely on monetary policy to keep the economy on an even keel. The Taylor Rule is a central component of modern thinking about how to deal with the business cycle. It has transformed monetary economics from an old-fashioned concern with monetary aggregates to an understanding that a rule itself can provide a nominal anchor to the economy. That's a tremendous step forward. The Taylor Rule gives policymakers a disciplined framework allowing economic stimulus when recessions strike while maintaining a credible promise to avoid later episodes of inflation. Monetary policy under the influence of the rule had delivered remarkably stable and low inflation over past decades, with only mild recessions, until the crisis hit.

The Taylor Rule instructs monetary policy to set a low federal funds interest rate to stimulate a soft economy. In 2008, prior to the crisis in September, the Federal Reserve Board had lowered the rate as the recession, which began in December 2007, took hold. Immediately after the crisis, in October 2008, the Fed lowered the funds rate almost all the way to its minimum possible value of zero. The question that has dogged monetary policy ever since is, "What do you do when the Taylor Rule tells you to set a negative Fed funds rate?" That's the central problem today. We can't just say, "Follow the Taylor Rule." There's a problem in the Taylor Rule, namely that the nominal interest rate cannot be less than zero. I'll address that issue later in the paper.

The result of this constraint on the Taylor Rule is that the interest rate is too high. The basic idea of modern monetary stabilization policy is to keep pushing the interest rate down until the economy is back at full employment, but that idea fails if a zero rate is still too high to regain full employment. When a really serious development causes a drastic reduction in the public's spending—as happened after the crisis—the Fed lacks the firepower of low interest rates to reverse the reduction and restore normal levels of spending, output, and employment. The inability to set rates low enough stymied the Fed during the Great Depression in the 1930s and has resulted in almost two decades of stagnation in Japan.

Inflation and interest rates push and pull the economy in different directions, so a discussion of interest rates needs to consider inflation as well. A low interest rate sends a signal to the public to spend now rather than later. A low rate implies a small reward to postponing spending by increasing saving and a small cost to spending now by borrowing. Similarly, a high rate of inflation rewards current spending by making the prices of goods purchased in the future higher than they are now. Normal monetary policy harnesses both forces in times of recession, by lowering the interest rate and nudging up the rate of inflation.

Recent monetary policy failed to deliver the usual stimulus on the inflation side as well as on the interest-rate side. Not only has the interest rate been stuck at a level just above zero, but inflation has declined by about 1 percent per year. The situation is nowhere nearly as bad as it was in the Depression, when prices fell rapidly and employment fell by more than 20 percent. Today, inflation seems remarkably unresponsive to conditions in the economy. Thus, the Fed cannot restore normal rates of inflation around 2 or 3 percent, but the Fed need not fear negative inflation, as in the Depression and in Japan over the past two decades.

The bottom line of all of this, and source of the most concern, is high and persistent unemployment resulting from the collapse of consumer spending following the crisis, uncorrected by normal monetary expansion. Unemployment reached its maximum value of 10.0 percent in October 2009 and declined gradually to 8.5 percent in December 2011. Forecasters don't have it reaching its normal range of 5 to 6 percent until around 2015, seven years after the crisis.

The Obama administration took command a few months after monetary policy had reached its limit of a zero interest rate and no corrective inflation. The new administration immediately announced an intention to use government purchases to correct the shortfall in private spending. Even in the two years when the Democrats controlled the House and the Senate as well as the presidency, the federal government was able to generate only modest increases in government purchases, while state and local purchases declined. I will discuss purchases and other spending policies later in this paper. There seems little inclination in Washington to enact further spending stimulus.

Given the exhaustion of monetary policy and the unwillingness to raise government spending, one wonders about the ability of any other policies to pull the economy out of the slump. At the end of the paper, I will address gimmicks—exotic, revenue-neutral, expansionary gimmicks. It's very frustrating being a macroeconomist today and knowing not one but two ways that, if policymakers would merely adopt them, could solve this problem overnight. They're revenue-neutral as well, and they don't involve any expansion of government spending. But this won't happen. When I dis-

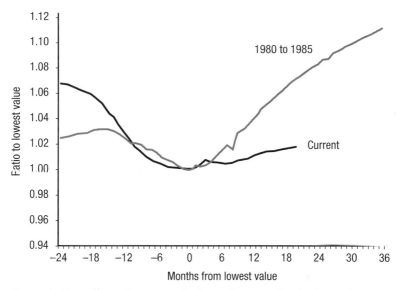

**Figure 1.** Payroll employment relative to lowest value in the cycle.

cuss them briefly at the end of this paper, you'll see that they're way too far out in left field—or right field, maybe—to be seriously considered.

## 2. Documenting the Persistent Slump

The most significant recession prior to the one that began at the end of 2007 was that of 1981–82. Figure 1 shows employment in that recession and recovery in comparison to the current slump. We're very far behind the expansionary path that was typical of recessions such as that of '81–'82. That problem has been addressed by me and others in recent research—see Hall (2011) and work cited there.

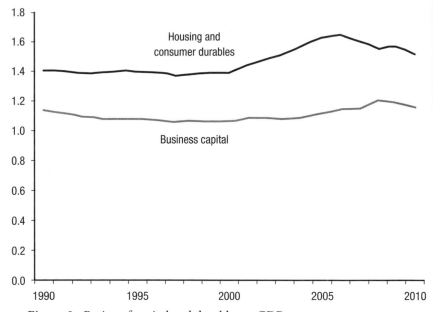

**Figure 2.** Ratios of capital and durables to GDP.
*Source:* U.S. National Income and Product Accounts, Fixed Asset Tables.

## 3. The Housing and Debt Binge Leading Up to the Crisis

In the 2000s, the United States was on a binge. We basically built a lot of houses and cars. The result was an overhang of household capital. Figure 2 documents the bulge of housing and consumer durables. It shows that the stock of housing and durables rose relative to GDP over the same years that the stock of business capital remained roughly constant relative to GDP. There have been a lot of stories about how interest rates were so low, or maybe too low, in the 2000s and that resulted in too much investment in general. But the investment was concentrated on the household side—residential and consumer durables. The figure shows that something special was affecting housing and durables but not affecting business capital. That something special was a substantial easing of lending standards to consumers, not matched by any similar easing of credit to businesses.

The stock of housing and consumer durables reached a peak right before the crash. A general principle of economics is that when one component of spending—here, spending on new houses and cars—rises for a period to abnormal levels, that component will fall back to normal or even fall below normal sometime soon. The overhang of household capital set the stage for part of the crash that occurred in late 2008, when both new home construction and auto production fell to shockingly low levels. But because those stocks gradually depreciate, the ratio of household capital to GDP is now beginning to decline. It's about halfway back to normal. Normal levels of home building and car production should resume once the elevated stocks from the past decade disappear. There's going to be a gradual improvement but it's very gradual.

## 4. Business Credit

The term "credit" refers to borrowing from financial institutions, mainly banks. An important fact about the United States is that most of GDP arises from non-credit-dependent businesses. This is not true in other economies, but it definitely differentiates the United States. Why is that? It's because the United States has a history of weak banking. The United States developed strong securities markets to offset weak banking, and that's been a good thing. It means that the impairment of banks from the crisis was not as harmful to businesses in the United States as it is elsewhere. In fact it hardly touched big businesses with direct access to securities markets such as Wal-Mart or Microsoft. Larger businesses, which account for the bulk of employment, have many alternative sources of finance besides bank loans. Of course, some sectors, such as transportation, are more credit-dependent, and smaller businesses cannot finance themselves from markets but, when they need to borrow, go to banks or bank-like financial institutions that suffered from the crisis.

## 5. Household Credit

Households have almost nowhere to turn for borrowing except banks and similar institutions. Unlike businesses, they cannot issue bonds or commercial paper and they certainly cannot issue equity. Thus the primary credit-dependent sector of the U.S. economy is the household. The wreckage from the financial crisis is found not in business but in the household. That's a very central finding of current research—see, in particular, Mian and Sufi (2011). Cutbacks in business spending were mostly a response to the collapse of household spending, not a direct result of the crisis.

A huge buildup of all kinds of consumer debt accompanied the binge of home building and car buying. First and foremost was mortgage debt, including the extension of mortgage borrowing to previously ineligible people through subprime lending. There was also a big accumulation of other types of debt; car loan debt and other kinds of debt expanded dramatically during the 2000s.

Many researchers, including myself, have been staring at the Survey of Consumer Finances recently and made the discovery that there's little liquidity protection for an ominous number of households (Kaplan and Violante (2011)). Here are some statistics for 2007, just before the crisis: Households illiquid by the standard of less than two months of liquid assets as a buffer, earned 58 percent of all income. That's not just people making $50,000 a year. If you look at the Survey of Consumer Finances, there are plenty of people making $400,000 a year who have no liquid assets at all. If they encounter something unexpected, like a smaller bonus, it has to come out of consumption, because they don't save their bonuses. If they did, they'd have liquid assets; but they don't. That's a remarkable fact. This involves more than three-quarters of all households, and many of these families are prosperous. By this standard, 74 percent of households are constrained. This is a big deal. The buffer comes from borrowing power and not from the holding of liquid assets. That's a very important thing to know about how the great majority of American families run their family finances.

The conclusion is that a substantial majority of households, which account for somewhat less than half of consumption, are dependent on financial institutions to sustain their standards of living in case of an interruption of income. When the crisis resulted in tighter lending standards, the majority of households needed to run tighter ships because they were aware that they had lost some of their access to lending and thus needed to be more conservative, especially in making commitments to high levels of committed payments (Guerrieri and Lorenzoni (2011)). Even more important, when their lenders cut their lines of credit for home equity and credit-card loans, they had to cut consumption to meet the lenders' demands for repayment. Both of these factors contributed to the large reduction in consumer spending that followed the crisis.

## 6. The Fragile Financial System

During the boom of the past decade, financial institutions became thinly capitalized. Leverage was extremely popular. The famous remark of CitiGroup's CEO, "As long as the music is playing, you've got to get up and dance,"[1] set the tone for the policies of major financial institutions. These institutions copied each other and became more and more precarious. They all thought it was safe because they didn't anticipate an unlikely event, the decline of housing prices.

There are two asset classes in the U.S. financial system broadly conceived. One is equity. Equity prices go up and down all the time. We had a huge decline in equity values in 2000, causing a mild recession. We have a robust equity-based system, and most business, as I mentioned before, is equity based. There's little leverage among equity holders, so a decline in equity values causes little stress and almost no cases of insolvency or bankruptcy. The government has never been called upon to bail out an institution funded mostly with equity.

On the other hand, we have the debt part of the financial system, which is based essentially entirely on real estate. It's very important to understand that. Basically, debt in the United States means real estate. It means, first of all, homeowners' mortgages, and then, all kinds of securities resting on mortgages. But it's all dependent on one asset class, namely real estate, which is vulnerable, as we discovered, to occasional substantial declines. Thinly capitalized institutions lost more than all their capital as a result of a modest decline in the underlying asset price, which was exclusively real estate. So that resulted in either failing or severely stressed financial institutions.

It's important to understand just how much of this distress remains today. All the major banks of the United States have suf-

---

1. *New York Times,* "Dealbook," July 10, 2007.

fered asset losses, according to the stock market. Bank of America and Citibank have market values of around 35 and 50 percent of book value, respectively.[2] The same thing is true in Europe. There are similar numbers for the French banks. Even the German banks are hurting, but not as badly. Thus we have an almost universal problem of financial institutions that are currently severely stressed.

These losses in asset value have resulted in a dramatic tightening of credit. The story in a nutshell is that a huge burst of home building and car buying, with the accompanying accumulation of debt, plus the tightening of credit standards, resulted in a collapse of spending on home building, consumer durables, and other categories of consumption. These declined sharply and remain low today. That's the basic story. It's a really simple story. And it's an ongoing one because problems in financial institutions and restrictions in the supply of credit to households remain in effect today. There's not been a lot of relaxation.

## 7. Indicators of Financial Stress

Figure 3 demonstrates the key fact of this paper. It shows the net money that the public was receiving from banks and other lenders (when above the horizontal line at zero) and the net money that the public was paying back to lenders (when below the horizontal line). The story is crystal clear. During the binge period from 2000 through 2006, families were playing a Ponzi game. They were borrowing more on a current basis than they were paying back in interest. They were financing all of the interest, and consumption

---

2. Source: finance.yahoo.com.

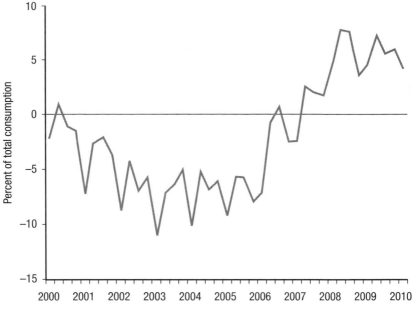

**Figure 3.** Burden of debt service.

*Source:* Author's calculations from Federal Reserve Board Flow of Funds and Loan Chargeoffs Data.

besides, by borrowing. Then at the beginning of the crisis, the flow changed dramatically. Starting in 2007, households paid cash back into financial institutions. This drain on household finances has continued right up to the present. The swing was about 20 percent of consumption. Families have been caught in a gigantic vise.

Another measure of tightening credit is the Senior Loan Officers Survey. Figure 4 shows an index of lending standards that I have calculated from the survey. The index shows that, especially with respect to mortgages, there was a huge increase in lending standards. The increase means it became more difficult for any

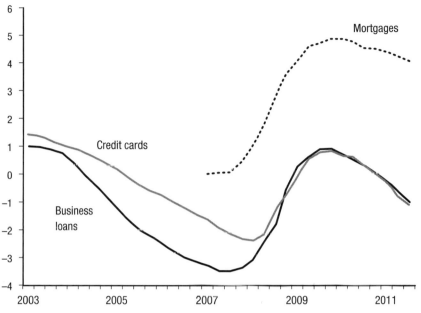

**Figure 4.** Indexes of lending standards inferred from the FRB Senior Loan Officer Survey.

*Source:* Author's calculations from Federal Reserve Board's Senior Loan Officers Survey.

given borrower with a given set of characteristics to be approved for a loan. The difficulty went way up and it's hardly gone down since then. Standards also became tougher for business loans, but in this sector there has been a good deal of relaxation. And the same is true of credit card lending standards. Mortgages are by far the biggest component of consumer credit, so the overall effect is still one of substantial tightening.

Google Insights is a valuable new tool for doing all kinds of research. It shows how the frequency of any popular search term

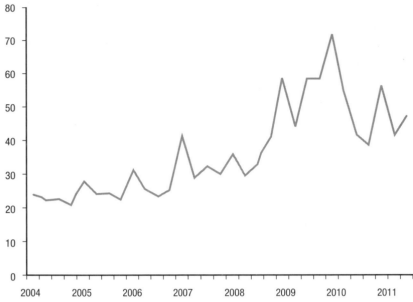

**Figure 5.** Indexes of Google search queries for the term "withdrawal penalty."

has changed over time. Figure 5 shows the volume of searches on the term "withdrawal penalty." This search term seemed best for documenting financial stress in households. Again, there's a huge increase starting at the end of 2007, coinciding exactly with the crisis, of people who had their backs to the wall sufficiently that they were searching the Internet for what to do about a withdrawal penalty. These people were considering taking money out of a long-term savings account or out of a retirement account, both moves that would only be chosen by those who no longer had access to more economical solutions to financial stress.

So those are the basics. We have families unable to spend as much. What effect would that have in an ordinary economy? Lower interest rates would stimulate consumption among families that are not liquidity-constrained. These families account for about half of all consumption. Business spending is interest sensitive, so it will increase when interest rates decline. If we could obey the Taylor Rule by setting a negative interest rate, then the shortfall of spending among constrained families would be offset by higher spending of unconstrained families and businesses. If the rate of minus 5 percent wasn't good enough, then we could go to minus 10 percent. Whatever the Taylor Rule tells us to do should work. But we can't do that. If the Taylor Rule requires a negative interest rate, the best we can do is a zero rate, which is inadequate to restore full employment.

## 8. Why Not Set Negative Interest Rates?

This is a good time to explain why we can't set negative interest rates. The reason is that the federal government, through the Federal Reserve, issues currency. Currency is a security that always has a zero nominal rate. It is the Fed's normal policy to allow the public to switch back and forth between currency and reserves whenever they want. The Fed is always standing ready to convert reserves to currency one to one. That's a fundamental principle of all central banks: to keep reserves and currency at par with each other. We don't even think about it, they do it so effectively. We don't think about there being separate markets for currency and for reserves because central banks are very efficient at pegging the two at the same value by swapping them back and forth as necessary. But because they do that, they would just find themselves with an infinite demand for currency if interest rates were negative, because currency would be a superior, dominant way of holding liquidity if the nominal rate became negative. That said, we are seeing more and more negative rates. Negative rates are becoming quite common in Europe now. They've occurred quite frequently in the secondary market for Treasury bills. If it were possible, it would be extremely desirable to run the economy according to the Taylor Rule, at a rate of perhaps minus five percent.

## 9. Inflation Won't Budge

I noted earlier that inflation could offset the impediment to monetary stimulus arising from the inability to achieve negative interest rates. A dose of, say, three points of added inflation would bring the same benefits as lowering the interest rate to minus 3 percent. Normally we think of the burden of inflation, but we live in a topsy-turvy world now. Unfortunately, there's nothing the Federal Reserve can do to affect the rate of inflation today. How do we know that? Because it's dying for more inflation. Inflation is too low. The Federal Reserve is a very well-run organization. It does not pass up opportunities to do what needs to be done. It's done everything it can to get inflation up. But inflation has been running at sub-par rates ever since the crisis began. We can't get inflation back up above 1.5 percent, which is where it's been running consistently since the crisis except for unexpected surges and declines, mostly from fuel prices.

Figure 6 shows the history of U.S. inflation since 1987, along with the unemployment rate. Inflation began the period at around 4 percent. It declined gradually until 1999 and remained remark-

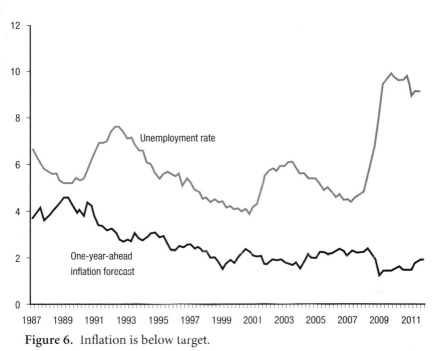

**Figure 6.** Inflation is below target.

ably close to 2 percent until the crisis, then dropped about 1 percent just after the crisis, and rose a bit recently. Ben Bernanke has identified 2 percent as the Fed's long-run goal for the inflation rate, so the rate still remains below target.

Alan Greenspan did a great job from 1987 to 2006 in completely stabilizing inflation. That accomplishment left a powerful anchor on inflation. Extreme slack in the economy has had almost no downward effect on inflation and heroic expansion of the Fed's portfolio has not succeeded in raising inflation. By contrast, in the Great Depression, a burst of unemployment resulted in the bottom falling out of the price level, and inflation got down to deeply negative territory. Nothing like that happened after the crisis of

2008. Some of us were afraid that it might, but it didn't. The flip side is the inability of the Fed to raise inflation up to its target rate of 2 percent.

## 10.  The Fed's Policy after It Exhausted Standard Interest-Rate Policy

The Fed lowered the interest rate to essentially zero immediately after the crisis. Since October 2008, the Fed has used another approach to expand the economy, aiming to raise output, lower unemployment, and raise inflation back to the target level. This approach—quantitative easing or QE—involves buying longer-term bonds and paying for them with reserves. Reserves are the way that the Fed borrows from banks. Because reserves have paid low but above-market interest rates throughout this period, banks willingly hold them. The Fed has become a gigantic hedge fund, borrowing from banks at 0.25 percent per year and investing in bonds that yield from 1 to 5 percent per year. So far, this "carry trade" has been highly profitable.

The first wave of bond-buying, QE1, involved mortgage-backed bonds. The Fed's intent was to buoy the housing market by increasing the demand and thus lowering the interest rate on the bonds. This policy appears to have been a success in the sense that mortgage-bond interest rates fell dramatically, and at least some of this benefit made its way into lower mortgage interest rates for home buyers.

The second wave of bond-buying, QE2, involved Treasury bonds. Krishnamurthy and Vissing-Jorgensen (2011) do a careful job of showing the noticeable but small effects of QE2. Table 1 shows that QE2 lowered rates on longer-term Treasury bonds by

**Table 1.** Effect of QE2 on bond interest rates.

| Security | Decline in interest rate, basis points |
|---|---|
| 30-year Treasury bond | 21 |
| 10-year Treasury note | 30 |
| 5-year Treasury note | 20 |
| 1-year Treasury bill | 1 |
| Long investment-grade corporate | 19 |
| Intermediate investment-grade corporate | 16 |
| Long junk corporate | 13 |
| Intermediate junk corporate | −17 |

*Note:* A basis point is 1/100 of a percentage point.
*Source:* Krishnamurthy and Vissing-Jorgensen (2011).

**Table 2.** Effect of QE2 on expected inflation.

| Inflation swap, years into future | Increase in expected future inflation, basis points |
|---|---|
| 30 | 4 |
| 10 | 4 |
| 5 | 4 |
| 1 | 5 |

*Note:* A basis point is 1/100 of a percentage point.
*Source:* Krishnamurthy and Vissing-Jorgensen (2011).

around a fifth of a percentage point. Rates on higher-quality corporate bonds fell by about the same amount, indicating that QE2 made funds cheaper for businesses and stimulated investment. The effects on lower-quality corporate bonds were ambiguous. Table 2 shows that QE2 had only tiny effects on expected inflation over both the short and long runs. The policy did almost nothing to get near-term inflation back up to target, so it was a disappointment in that sense. On the other hand—contrary to the beliefs of some critics—the policy did almost nothing to kindle worries that the huge expansion in the Fed's issuance of reserves might result in higher inflation in the longer run.

In normal times and under historical policy, if the Fed expanded its portfolio as much as it has since the crisis, the effect would have been extremely expansionary and inflationary. The Fed's critics are concerned that as soon as the economy begins to return to normal, inflation will take off. Obviously markets don't agree with the critics, or else the QE policies would have raised expectations of inflation in the longer run, and Table 2 shows that this did not happen. The reason that markets are right and the critics are wrong is that the Fed plans to contract its portfolio when the time comes to start raising interest rates. Moreover, the Fed has put in place a new policy never used historically—it is now paying interest on reserves and it can maintain banks' willingness to hold high levels of reserves by increasing the rate it pays on them.

## 11. Spending Policy

Both the Bush and Obama administrations cranked up government spending in response to the recession that began at the end of 2007 and intensified after the crisis in late 2008. Government spending has two components that often play roles in offsetting weakness in the economy: (1) purchases of goods and services, and (2) transfers that boost people's incomes. Figure 7 shows what happened to purchases measured by combining two layers of government: federal and state-local. The lines show the volume of purchases adjusted for inflation and for normal upward trends. Federal purchases rose rapidly in the last year of the Bush

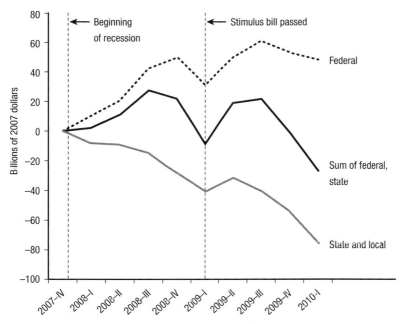

**Figure 7.** Spending policy: government purchases.
*Source:* Hall (2010).

administration, plunged at the changeover in the first quarter of 2009, recovered in the second quarter, then rose but not as rapidly under Obama as under Bush. Although Obama's stimulus bill passed in the first quarter, the data show no signs of any large growth as a result of the bill. State and local purchases declined sharply over the period, so total government purchases declined modestly. Government as a whole made no contribution to stimulus from higher purchases over the period shown. Some critics of using government purchases to stimulate the economy have said that the policy failed, but what they mean is that it was never tried.

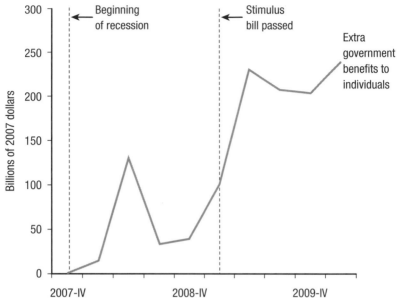

**Figure 8.** Spending policy: transfers.
*Source:* Hall (2010).

The story of government transfers—unemployment compensation, food stamps, and other types of income support—shown in Figure 8, is entirely different. Again, the line is adjusted for inflation and normal growth. I do not break down transfers between federal and state-local because many transfer programs receive funds from both levels. The government was successful in putting almost a quarter of a trillion dollars of extra income in the hands of the public. Part of the increase came from programs that automatically expand in bad times, such as unemployment compensation and food stamps, and part from expansions of programs,

**Table 3.** Effects of spending policy.

|  | *Purchases* | *Transfers* | *Total* |
|---|---|---|---|
| Average federal stimulus, 2009Q2–2010Q1 | 58 | 220 | |
| Multiplier | 2 | 0.8 | |
| Effect | 115 | 176 | 291 |
| GDP | | | 14,338 |
| Percent of GDP | 0.8 | 1.2 | 2.0 |
| Average GDP shortfall | | | 8.2 |
| Counterfactual GDP shortfall | | | 10.2 |

*Source:* Hall (2010).

notably the extension of unemployment benefits to the long-term unemployed who do not receive support in normal times.

Table 3 gives rough estimates of the effects of spending policy over the period from the second quarter of 2009 through the first quarter of 2010, at annual rates. The figures for purchases consider only the federal government, which raised purchases by $58 billion. I estimate that the multiplier under the conditions of that period was two dollars of added GDP for each dollar of added federal purchases. Recent research has confirmed that the purchases multiplier is substantially higher in times when the interest rate is pinned at zero than in times when the Fed adjusts it according to its Taylor Rule—see Christiano, Eichenbaum, and Rebelo (2011). In normal times the multiplier is somewhat less than one, but is around two when the Taylor Rule is inoperative. The increase in transfers was much larger, but the multiplier effect of transfers is quite a bit smaller, around 0.8, because families use transfers to pay down debts as well as to buy goods and services. I estimate that the combined effect of the two types of spending expansion raised GDP by about two percentage points. The policy prevented an even worse contraction of GDP than actually occurred.

## A Choice of Magic Bullets

Finally, let me conclude with not one but two magic bullets. We need to send a message to people that the best time to spend is now. What's wrong with the economy is that consumers are looking around and saying, "I can't borrow, I've all these reasons. So I really shouldn't spend now. I'm going to spend later." But with unused resources, we want the signal to be: spend now! A negative interest rate would do exactly that. A negative interest rate would say you'll lose money if you defer, so spend now. But since we can't have a negative interest rate, we can do something which has the same effect, which is we can use taxes to send the message that it's better to spend now than later. Value-added or sales taxes can be manipulated to make consumption cheaper now than later. Martin Feldstein initiated this idea in 2003 in the Japanese context. Correia, Farhi, Nicolini, and Teles (2011) have picked up the ball. All we need to do is to announce today a phase-in of a national sales or value-added tax. Because the public would know that the rate would grow over time, the tax would make current consumption cheap relative to future consumption. For example, if the tax rate rose 5 percentage points per year, it would be equivalent to have an inflation rate 5 percentage points per year, say 7 percent rather than 2 percent. At the same time, there would be a phase-out of the income tax by the same amount per year, so the tax change would have little effect on the total tax bill.

So if the Taylor Rule indicates minus 5 percent, that says we should raise the consumption tax rate 5 percent per year. We probably need a consumption tax in the 20–25 percent range, which would allow a phase-in over four or five years. As soon as we announced that, it would transform the economy. We could have a new kind of Taylor Rule. When it runs out of power with the Fed funds rate, it just switches to changing the rate of change of the consumption tax rate. As a long-time advocate of consumption taxes, I maintain there's a double benefit here, because switching to a consumption tax is a great idea on its own merits. Notice that a changeover from an income to a consumption tax can and should be revenue-neutral—this plan does not involve any increase in the deficit. Rather, the expansion it would ignite would raise revenue, cut spending on benefits, and lower the deficit dramatically.

The second magic bullet operates in the monetary sphere. Earlier I explained that the existence of currency is the root cause of the Fed's inability to set negative interest rates. So a second idea is that the Fed should just stop exchanging reserves for currency at par. To exchange reserves for currency at par in a negative interest-rate environment is to create a federal security that dominates all others. It pays above market return, namely zero when the market return is negative. There's no reason why we have to do that. All we need to do is have the two float against each other. If we did that, then the price of currency relative to stated prices, and relative to reserves in particular, would jump upward. There would be a currency shortage, which would be solved by the price system by an upward jump in the value of the currency. Then, from that point on, the price of the currency would decline over time at whatever the prevailing negative nominal interest rate was. This would give equilibrium in asset markets, because the nominal return on currency would now be minus 5 percent, instead of being locked at zero, because the price of currency would float. The world would change in one rather surprising way: if you went to the ATM and took $30 out of your bank account, the ATM machine would give you only $20 because the price of dollars relative to reserves had appreciated to that level.

So that's the second answer—probably the first one is more practical. But the point is we have two gimmick answers, not just one. And it seems that at some point we ought to start thinking about this issue, because this paralysis of monetary policy, the inability to follow the Taylor Rule, is a serious impediment to proper policymaking. It's the source of the persistence of the slump in the U.S. economy.

## References

Christiano, Lawrence J., Martin Eichenbaum, and Sergio Rebelo, "When Is the Government Spending Multiplier Large?" *Journal of Political Economy,* February 2011, 119 (1), 78–121.

Correia, Isabel, Emmanuel Farhi, Juan Pablo Nicolini, and Pedro Teles, "Unconventional Fiscal Policy at the Zero Bound," October 2011.

Guerrieri, Veronica and Guido Lorenzoni, "Credit Crises, Precautionary Savings and the Liquidity Trap," October 2011. University of Chicago Booth School of Business.

Hall, Robert E., "Fiscal Stimulus," *Daedalus,* 2010, Fall, 83–94.

———, "The Long Slump," *American Economic Review,* April 2011, 101 (2), 431–69. 2011 AEA Presidential Address.

Kaplan, Greg and Giovanni L. Violante, "A Model of the Consumption Response to Fiscal Stimulus Payments," September 2011. University of Pennsylvania.

Krishnamurthy, Arvind and Annette Vissing-Jorgensen, "The Effects of Quantitative Easing on Interest Rates: Channels and Implications for Policy," *Brookings Papers on Economic Activity,* 2011, (2). Forthcoming.

Mian, Atif and Amir Sufi, "What Explains High Unemployment? The Aggregate Demand Channel," November 2011. University of Chicago Booth School of Business.

# CHAPTER 5

# What the Government Purchases Multiplier Actually Multiplied in the 2009 Stimulus Package

JOHN F. COGAN AND JOHN B. TAYLOR*

The debate about the impact of the American Recovery and Reinvestment Act of 2009 (ARRA) has been accompanied by a surge of research on the size of the government purchases multiplier. In a recent review of model simulations and empirical studies, Ramey (2011) finds that the range of estimates of the "multiplier for a *temporary, deficit-financed* increase in government *purchases* . . . is probably between 0.8 and 1.5," adding that, "Reasonable people can argue, however, that the data do not reject 0.5 or 2."[1]

In order to evaluate the impact of ARRA on the economy, however, one needs to know what the government purchases multiplier actually multiplied in the case of ARRA—that is, the change in government purchases due to ARRA. Even for extremely large values of the multiplier, the impact on GDP and employment would be very small through this channel if ARRA did not increase gov-

---

* The authors thank Cynthia Liu and Sam Shapiro for very helpful research assistance.

1. The government purchases multiplier is the increase in Gross Domestic Product resulting from a $1 increase in government expenditures on goods and services.

ernment purchases by very much. The purpose of this paper is to estimate the actual change in government purchases due to ARRA, both at the federal and at the state and local level. We use a new data series on the direct effects of ARRA on federal government purchases and on grants to state and local governments.

Because the ARRA grants to state and local government are fungible and not synchronized with purchases, determining the effect of ARRA on state and local government purchases is more difficult and uncertain than determining the effect on federal government purchases. We therefore analyze the state and local purchases data in detail. We trace where the money went since ARRA began, estimate time-series regressions of the relationship between ARRA grants and state and local government purchases, and consider a counterfactual. Our main finding is that the increase in government purchases due to the ARRA has been remarkably small, especially when compared to the large size of the overall ARRA package. In fact, the effect of ARRA on purchases appears to be so small that the size of the government purchases multiplier does not matter much compared to many other factors affecting the growth of GDP. We compare our findings on the 2009 stimulus with research by Gramlich (1979) on a similar countercyclical program in the 1970s and find the results to be remarkably similar.

## 1. The Multiplier Debate and the Importance of Data on Government Purchases

The recent resurgence in the debate over the size of the government purchases multiplier began in January 2009, when Romer and Bernstein (2009) released a paper showing that the multiplier was around 1.5 and that the stimulus package would have a large effect. Then, in February 2009, Cogan, Cwik, Taylor, and Wieland

(2010) issued a working paper arguing that the results of Romer and Bernstein (2009) were unlikely to be robust because they excluded simulations from more modern "new Keynesian" models, where the multiplier in the case of ARRA was much smaller— around .5 as illustrated with a model based on Smets and Wouters (2007) and Christiano, Eichenbaum, and Evans (2005).

These papers were followed by a series of papers using new Keynesian models, including Christiano, Eichenbaum, and Rebelo (2011), Eggertsson (2010), Erceg and Linde (2009), Hall (2009), and Drautzburg and Uhlig (2010). While the multipliers differed somewhat among the new Keynesian models, Woodford (2010) showed they were quite similar once one controlled for timing differences. More recently, Coenen et al. (2012) calculated and compared the government purchases multipliers from seven estimated new Keynesian models used for policy evaluation at the Bank of Canada, the Federal Reserve Board (two models), the European Central Bank, the European Commission, the International Monetary Fund, and the Organization for Economic Cooperation and Development (OECD) plus the models of Cogan, Cwik, Taylor, and Wieland (2010) and Christiano, Eichenbaum, and Evans (2005). This study found that the government purchases multiplier was on average about the same size as that presented in Cogan, Cwik, Taylor, and Wieland (2010).

As Hall (2009) has emphasized the government purchases multiplier that has been the subject of this debate is the change in GDP associated with a change in government *purchases*—or simply the $G$ in $C+I+G+X$. Government purchases are much different from government expenditures. Government purchases do not include transfer payments, subsidies, and interest payments, which are all part of government expenditures. The best source of data on government purchases for macroeconomic purposes is the quarterly national income and product accounts (NIPA). Throughout this paper we use seasonally adjusted quarterly NIPA data stated at annual rates.

Government purchases in the NIPA are divided into two major components: consumption expenditures and gross investment. Consumption expenditures consist of goods and services produced for public consumption such as law enforcement services, national defense, and elementary and secondary education.[2] Gross investment includes purchases of new structures, equipment, and software. The NIPA also breaks down government purchases into two sectors: (1) federal and (2) state and local. The federal sector is further broken down into defense and non-defense.

In addition to the NIPA data, the Bureau of Economic Analysis (BEA) provides quarterly data on the effect of ARRA on federal government sector transactions in the NIPA. The data are updated each month at the time of the advance estimates and updates of quarterly GDP in "Effect of the ARRA on Selected Federal Government Sector Transactions," which is posted on the BEA website at http://www.bea.gov/recovery/index.htm?tabContainer Main=1.

The BEA data focus on the federal sector and thus give the amount of ARRA that is in the form of federal government purchases—both consumption and gross investment. From these data the effect of ARRA on federal government purchases can be determined in a straightforward manner.

It is more difficult, however, to determine the effect of ARRA on state and local government purchases. The BEA reports the amount of ARRA that is in the form of current grants to state

---

2. Government consumption expenditures also include consumption of fixed capital, a partial measure of the value of the services from fixed government capital.

and local governments for Medicaid, education, and other items as well as capital grants to state and local governments for roads, bridges, and other public infrastructure projects. However, the BEA does not report whether or how these funds were used to purchase goods and services. In the next section we present the results for federal government purchases and in the following section we consider the impact at the state and local level.

## Effect of ARRA on Federal Government Purchases

Table 1 shows the effect of ARRA on total federal government purchases as a percentage of GDP starting in the first quarter of 2009 when ARRA began. It also shows the act's impact on the two main components of government purchases—government consumption and government gross investment.

**Table 1.** Effect of ARRA on federal government purchases, federal government consumption, and federal government gross investment as a percentage of GDP.

|        | *Federal Government Purchases* | *Federal Government Consumption* | *Federal Gross Investment* |
|--------|:---:|:---:|:---:|
| 2009Q1 | 0.00 | 0.00 | 0.00 |
| 2009Q2 | 0.01 | 0.01 | 0.00 |
| 2009Q3 | 0.11 | 0.09 | 0.02 |
| 2009Q4 | 0.10 | 0.09 | 0.01 |
| 2010Q1 | 0.12 | 0.11 | 0.02 |
| 2010Q2 | 0.15 | 0.12 | 0.03 |
| 2010Q3 | 0.19 | 0.14 | 0.05 |
| 2010Q4 | 0.15 | 0.11 | 0.04 |
| 2011Q1 | 0.13 | 0.09 | 0.04 |
| 2011Q2 | 0.12 | 0.09 | 0.03 |
| 2011Q3 | 0.12 | 0.08 | 0.04 |

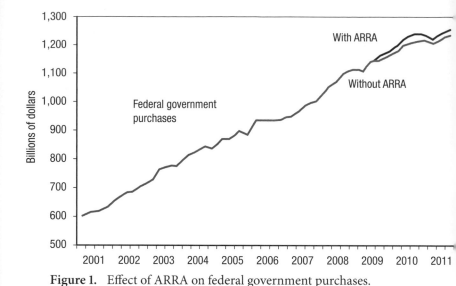

**Figure 1.** Effect of ARRA on federal government purchases.

Note that the impact of ARRA on federal purchases built up gradually during 2009 and 2010, and did not reach a peak until the third quarter of 2010. However, the impact never amounted to more than a very small percentage of GDP. At its peak, ARRA increased federal government purchases by only .19 percent of GDP and federal infrastructure spending by only .05 percent of GDP.

Figure 1 illustrates the effect of ARRA compared with the overall trend and the fluctuations in federal purchases since 2000. It shows, at annual rates, federal government purchases with and without the effect of ARRA. While clearly visible in the graph, the impact of ARRA is no larger than many of the other short-run fluctuations in federal purchases over this period.

Of the total stimulus package—originally estimated to be $862 billion in size—the amount allocated to federal government purchases was $7.5 billion in 2009 and $22.2 in 2010 according to the BEA data. The portion allocated to infrastructure investment at the federal level was $0.9 billion in 2009 and $4.8 billion in 2010. Clearly these amounts are too small to be a material part of the changes in real GDP growth during the recent recovery, even if the multiplier were quite large.

## 2. Effects of ARRA on State and Local Government Purchases

A key feature of the ARRA is that it provided large transfers to state and local governments in the form of grants-in-aid. For the purposes of assessing the impact of ARRA on GDP, it is important to distinguish between two types of grants. First are those that state and local governments may directly use to finance purchases of goods and services. Grants for transportation projects and elementary and secondary schools are included in this category. The second type consists of transfers that supplement household resources. Federal Medicaid grants to states fall into this category. Under NIPA accounting conventions, state Medicaid expenditures are treated as transfer payments to households which raise their disposable personal income. Their impact on GDP depends on how much of the rise in income results in a rise in personal consumption expenditures. In addition, to the extent that higher federal Medicaid grants are fungible at the state level they may free up other state revenues, and their impact may also be reflected by higher state government purchases of goods and services.

Table 2 shows the amount of ARRA grants, expressed in annual rates and as a percentage of GDP. Except for the first half of 2009, a majority of the grants are for areas other than Medicaid. The total grants to state and local governments rose to .9 percent of GDP by the third quarter of 2010 and then start to taper off.

**Table 2.** ARRA federal transfers (grants) to state and local governments (billions of dollars at annual rates and percent of GDP).

|        |       |          |       | Percentage of GDP | | |
|--------|-------|----------|-------|-------|----------|-------|
|        | Total | Medicaid | Other | Total | Medicaid | Other |
| 2009Q1 | 49.4  | 48.9     | 0.5   | 0.36  | 0.35     | 0.00  |
| 2009Q2 | 73.4  | 39.1     | 34.3  | 0.53  | 0.28     | 0.25  |
| 2009Q3 | 90.4  | 38.4     | 52.0  | 0.65  | 0.28     | 0.37  |
| 2009Q4 | 102.9 | 38.9     | 64.0  | 0.73  | 0.28     | 0.45  |
| 2010Q1 | 117.2 | 51.7     | 65.5  | 0.82  | 0.36     | 0.46  |
| 2010Q2 | 128.6 | 40.9     | 87.7  | 0.89  | 0.28     | 0.61  |
| 2010Q3 | 131.5 | 42.7     | 88.8  | 0.90  | 0.29     | 0.61  |
| 2010Q4 | 120.6 | 48.4     | 72.2  | 0.82  | 0.33     | 0.49  |
| 2011Q1 | 62.7  | 4.3      | 58.4  | 0.42  | 0.03     | 0.39  |
| 2011Q2 | 62.5  | 1.8      | 60.7  | 0.42  | 0.01     | 0.40  |
| 2011Q3 | 44.3  | 2.1      | 42.2  | 0.29  | 0.01     | 0.28  |

ARRA grants are treated as part of total receipts or aggregate income of the state and local government sector. Figure 2 shows total receipts with and without the ARRA grants. These ARRA grants reached a peak of 6 percent of total state and local government income in the third quarter of 2010 before declining.

## The Budget Constraint for State and Local Governments

The important question is what effect these grants had on government purchases at the state and local level. To answer this we must consider how state and local governments respond to these grants. We view the response of state and local governments as somewhat analogous to how the household sector responds to changes in transfer payments by adjusting consumption, where permanent income or life-cycle models have proved useful and accurate. As in the household sector, state and local government officials rec-

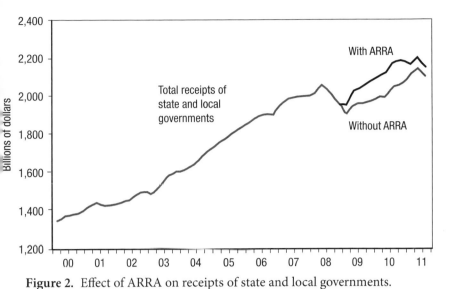

**Figure 2.** Effect of ARRA on receipts of state and local governments.

ognize that the grants are temporary. And as in the household sector, state and local governments can use federal grants for other purposes than purchases of goods and services. Depending on the timing and the degree to which ARRA grants are fungible, state and local governments could borrow less, save more, or increase expenditures on "non-purchase" items such as transfer payments to individuals. And of course, the incentives and constraints facing state and local governments may be more complex than those of households, which may make the permanent income theory less valid.

The budget constraint for the state and local government sector helps frame the issues. The following variables[3] refer to the state and local sector in the aggregate:

---

3. Each variable has an exact counterpart in the NIPA accounts. In BEA Table 3.3, the variable $G$ is Line 22 plus Line 35. The variable $E$ is Line 33 less $G$. $L$ is Line 39. $A$

$G_t$ = government purchases
$E_t$ = expenditures other than government purchases
$L_t$ = net lending or net borrowing $(-)$
$R_t$ = receipts other than ARRA grants
$A_t$ = ARRA grants

The budget constraint facing state and local governments is

$$G_t + E_t + L_t = R_t + A_t \tag{1}$$

The key question is how much an increase in ARRA grants $A_t$ resulted in an increase in state and local government purchases $G_t$. Note that, depending on various constraints and expectations, an increase in $A_t$ could also affect other expenditures $E_t$ or loans/borrowings $L_t$.

## The Lack of a Response in Government Purchases to ARRA

Figure 3 shows the pattern of state and local government purchases from 2000 to the third quarter of 2011. One critical fact stands out in this figure: state and local government purchases declined sharply in the fourth quarter of 2008 and remained remarkably flat for two years. There is no noticeable increase in government purchases during the period of the ARRA grants. Not until the

---

is the ARRA component of Line 20 plus Line 28 of the BEA publication "Effect of the ARRA on Selected Federal Government Sector Transactions." The variable $R$ is line 30 of Table 3.3 less $A$. Note that total expenditures (Line 33 of Table 3.3) include net purchases of "non-produced assets" and exclude consumption of fixed capital. These series are also consistent with the state and local sector of the Federal Reserve's flow of funds accounts. Net lending or net borrowing equals net financial investment minus the statistical discrepancy due to the difference between data on acquisition of financial assets/liabilities and income/expenditure data.

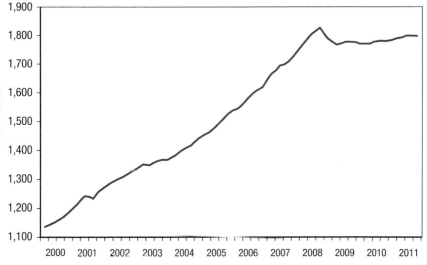

**Figure 3.** State and local government purchases: 2000Q1–2011Q3.

first quarter of 2011, did they pass the level reached in the fourth quarter of 2008.

The timing and magnitude of these income and spending changes are shown in more detail in Table 3, which focuses on the period of the ARRA starting in the first quarter of 2009. The table shows the *change* in state and local government spending and receipts from fourth quarter 2008 levels. The first column shows receipts excluding the ARRA grants. The effect of the recession on state and local income is clear. As the data in column 1 show, state and local receipts declined sharply in the first quarter of 2009 and they then began to rebound, passing the 2008Q4 level by 2009Q4.

The change in state and local government purchases from the level in the fourth quarter of 2008 is presented in column 2. Government purchases show no appreciable rebound until 2011 despite the receipt of ARRA grants starting in early 2009. The

**Table 3.** Change in receipts and purchases of goods and services from 2008Q4 level (billions of dollars at annual rates).

|         | Receipts ex ARRA | Purchases | ARRA grants ex Medicaid | Receipts ex Medicaid |
|---------|-----------------:|----------:|------------------------:|---------------------:|
| 2009Q1  | −58.8            | −19.8     | 0.5                     | −58.3                |
| 2009Q2  | −18.7            | −10.2     | 34.3                    | 15.6                 |
| 2009Q3  | −6.3             | −12.6     | 52.0                    | 45.7                 |
| 2009Q4  | 9.1              | −17.8     | 64.0                    | 73.1                 |
| 2010Q1  | 19.8             | −17.3     | 65.5                    | 85.3                 |
| 2010Q2  | 32.1             | −9.8      | 87.7                    | 119.8                |
| 2010Q3  | 78.0             | −8.7      | 88.8                    | 166.8                |
| 2010Q4  | 101.8            | −3.9      | 72.2                    | 174.0                |
| 2011Q1  | 141.5            | 4.6       | 58.4                    | 199.9                |
| 2011Q2  | 180.6            | 11.6      | 60.7                    | 241.3                |
| 2011Q3  | 138.0            | 8.9       | 42.2                    | 180.2                |

ARRA grants are shown in column 3 and exclude Medicaid grants, reflecting the assumption that Medicaid grants are not fungible. The non-Medicaid ARRA grants begin in the first quarter of 2009 and flow into state and local governments in larger amounts as time progresses. By the third quarter of 2009, the non-Medicaid ARRA grants reach over $50 billion on an annualized basis and continue rising. But, as Table 3 makes very clear, state and local government purchases show no response.[4]

## Where Did the Money Go?

The data presented in Table 3 raise the question: if the ARRA grants to states were not spent by state and local governments on

---

4. Including Medicaid grants in receipts reinforces this point. Under the alternative assumption that Medicaid grants are fungible and, hence would be included in state and local receipts available to finance purchases, the total ARRA grants received in 2010 rise to $103 billion and $127 billion in the first two quarters, respectively.

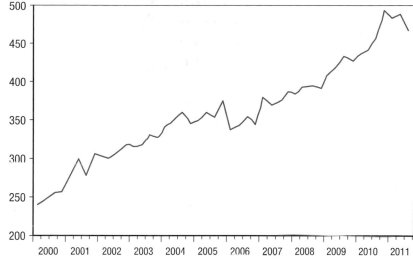

**Figure 4.** State and local government expenditures other than for purchases of goods and services: 2000Q1–2011Q3.

increased purchases of goods and services, how were these grants spent? Assuming that tax codes are not changed in response to ARRA, the budget constraint (equation 1) allows for only two other possibilities: higher expenditures on "non-purchase" activities and lower borrowing. Figures 4 and 5 provide some indication of each of these alternatives.

Figure 4 shows that state and local government "non-purchase" expenditures kept growing without any slowdown. The pace of their growth appears to have picked up around the time that the ARRA grants began. Note also that the growth declined around the time that ARRA grants began to taper off.

The data in Table 4 focus on the period of the ARRA and confirm these graphical observations. Column 1 shows the change in non-purchase expenditures from the level in the fourth quarter of 2008 to each subsequent quarter. Non-purchase expenditures rise at an almost unbroken rate and, by the fourth quarter of

**Table 4.** Change in receipts and non-purchase expenditures from 2008Q4 level (billions of dollars at annual rates).

| | Non-Purchase Expenditures | ARRA Grants |
|---|---|---|
| 2009Q1 | 17.7 | 49.4 |
| 2009Q2 | 27.4 | 73.4 |
| 2009Q3 | 40.0 | 90.4 |
| 2009Q4 | 35.0 | 102.9 |
| 2010Q1 | 44.9 | 117.2 |
| 2010Q2 | 49.6 | 128.6 |
| 2010Q3 | 66.5 | 131.5 |
| 2010Q4 | 101.2 | 120.6 |
| 2011Q1 | 92.5 | 62.7 |
| 2011Q2 | 96.7 | 62.5 |
| 2011Q3 | 74.7 | 44.3 |

2010, they are 26 percent higher than they were two years earlier. This increase stands in sharp contrast to the decline in state and local purchases. As the table also shows, the rise and fall of non-purchase expenditures correspond quite closely to the rise and fall of ARRA grants, shown in column 2.

Figure 5 shows the pattern of state and local net lending or net borrowing, the remaining area that could be impacted by ARRA grants. As the chart shows, although state and local governments have on average been borrowing in recent years, there have been large swings. Borrowing increased sharply after the dot com bubble burst in 2000 and did not start falling again until 2003, long after the recovery from the 2001 recession began. Borrowing increased again as the housing bubble burst, but then started turning around before the recession was over, much earlier than in the previous recession.

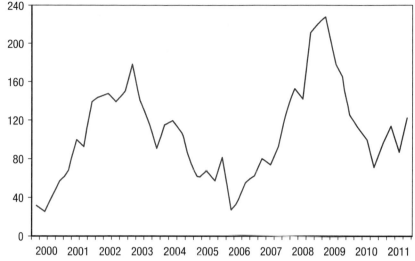

**Figure 5.** Net borrowing by state and local governments:
2000Q1–2011Q3.

Table 5 shows the behavior of total state and local net lending
and its relation to ARRA receipts during the current recession. As
with Tables 3 and 4, the amounts are the changes from 2008Q4.
Column 1 shows total state and local expenditures. Columns 2, 3,
and 4 show state and local receipts excluding ARRA grants, ARRA
grants, and total receipts, respectively. Column 5 shows net lending, simply the difference between column 1 and column 4.

An inspection of these data suggests that the ARRA grants
to state and local governments were closely associated with an
increase in net lending or, equivalently, a decrease in the rate of
borrowing. As ARRA grants increased, so did net lending; as
ARRA grants tapered off, so did net lending. Indeed, the peak in
net lending occurred in precisely the same quarter as the peak in

**Table 5.** Change in receipts and net lending from 2008Q4 level (billions of dollars at annual rates).

|  | Total Expenditures | Receipts ex ARRA | ARRA Grants | Total Receipts | Net Lending |
|---|---|---|---|---|---|
| 2009Q1 | −2.1 | −58.8 | 49.4 | −9.4 | −7.3 |
| 2009Q2 | 17.2 | −18.7 | 73.4 | 54.7 | 37.6 |
| 2009Q3 | 27.4 | −6.3 | 90.4 | 84.1 | 56.6 |
| 2009Q4 | 17.2 | 9.1 | 102.9 | 112.0 | 94.8 |
| 2010Q1 | 27.6 | 19.8 | 117.2 | 137.0 | 109.4 |
| 2010Q2 | 39.8 | 32.1 | 128.6 | 160.7 | 120.9 |
| 2010Q3 | 57.8 | 78.0 | 131.5 | 209.5 | 151.8 |
| 2010Q4 | 97.3 | 101.8 | 120.6 | 222.4 | 125.1 |
| 2011Q1 | 97.1 | 141.5 | 62.7 | 204.2 | 107.1 |
| 2011Q2 | 108.3 | 180.6 | 62.5 | 243.1 | 134.8 |
| 2011Q3 | 83.6 | 138.0 | 44.3 | 182.3 | 98.8 |

ARRA grants. In contrast, there was no such association with the change in government purchases during the period of ARRA.

## Time Series Regression Estimates of the Impact of ARRA

Simple time series regression techniques can also be used to estimate the impact of ARRA grants at the state and local level. Using the notation previously introduced, we consider the following three equations:

$$G_t = a_0 + a_1 G_{t-1} + a_2 R_t + a_3 A_t \tag{2}$$

$$E_t = b_0 + b_1 E_{t-1} + b_2 R_t + b_3 A_t \tag{3}$$

$$L_t = c_0 + c_1 G_{t-1} + c_2 E_{t-1} + c_3 R_t + c_4 A_t \tag{4}$$

Equation (2) describes how government purchases responds to ARRA grants and to receipts other than ARRA grants. The lagged dependent variable allows for the possibility that purchases respond with a lag to changes in income, much as an estimated consumption function for households includes lagged consumption to portray such lags. Equation (3) for non-purchases expenditures is of the same functional form.

The state and local budget constraint (1) along with equations (2) and (3) imply equation (4) for net lending. The relationship between the coefficients in equation (4) and the coefficients in equations (2) and (3) can be obtained by substituting equations (2) and (3) into equation (1). This gives

$$L_t = R_t + A_t - a_0 - a_1 G_{t-1} - a_2 R_t - a_3 A_t - b_0 - b_1 E_{t-1} - b_2 R_t - b_3 A_t$$
$$= -(a_0 + b_0) - a_1 G_{t-1} - b_1 E_{t-1} + (1 - a_2 - b_2) R_t + (1 - a_3 - b_3) A_t \quad (5)$$

which implies the following identities:

$$c_0 = -(a_0 + b_0) \quad\quad\quad\quad\quad\quad\quad\quad\quad\quad\quad\quad\quad (6)$$

$$c_1 = -a_1 \quad\quad\quad\quad\quad\quad\quad\quad\quad\quad\quad\quad\quad\quad\quad\quad (7)$$

$$c_2 = -b_1 \quad\quad\quad\quad\quad\quad\quad\quad\quad\quad\quad\quad\quad\quad\quad\quad (8)$$

$$c_3 = (1 - a_2 - b_2) \quad\quad\quad\quad\quad\quad\quad\quad\quad\quad\quad\quad (9)$$

$$c_4 = (1 - a_3 - b_3) \quad\quad\quad\quad\quad\quad\quad\quad\quad\quad\quad (10)$$

We estimated equations (2), (3), and (4) subject to the constraints in equations (6) through (10) by least squares over the period from

**Table 6.** Estimated regression coefficients for the equations for government purchases ($G$), non-purchase expenditures ($E$), and net lending ($L$) as a function of total receipts less ARRA grants ($R$) and ARRA grants ($A$). Sample 1969Q1–2011Q3. In the parentheses are t-statistics computed from Newey-West (1987) estimated standard errors.

|  | Dependent Variable | | |
|---|---|---|---|
|  | $G$ | $E$ | $L$ |
| Constant | 3.659 | −6.100 | 2.442 |
|  | [3.863] | [−4.809] | [ 1.919] |
| $G(-1)$ | 0.876 |  | −0.876 |
|  | [57.880] |  | [−57.880] |
| $E(-1)$ |  | 0.743 | −0.743 |
|  |  | [24.716] | [−24.716] |
| $R$ | 0.113 | 0.0559 | 0.831 |
|  | [8.864] | [8.681] | [58.680] |
| $A$ | −0.0967 | 0.163 | 0.933 |
|  | [−3.495] | [5.832] | [30.730] |
| $R^2$ | 0.999 | 0.997 | 0.958 |

1969Q1 to 2011Q3. An inspection of the residuals of the estimated equations showed some serial correlation and heteroskedasticity which differed from equation to equation, so we computed the standard errors of the estimated coefficients in each equation with a heteroskedasticity auto-correlation consistent (HAC) method due to Newey and West (1987). The estimated coefficients along with t-statistics using these standard errors are reported in Table 6.

Observe that there is a very large and significant effect of ARRA grants on net lending. The coefficient on ARRA grants is .93, quite close to one. Thus, these regression results are consistent with the findings from the graphical and numerical analysis presented above that states and localities used ARRA grants primarily to reduce their borrowing. Note also that the coefficient on

ARRA grants in the government purchases equation is negative and statistically different from zero, while the coefficient on ARRA grants in the non-purchase expenditures equation is positive and statistically different from zero. Taken together, the two coefficients imply that ARRA had a relatively small impact on total state and local government expenditures but shifted these expenditures away from purchases toward transfers.

## Why the Widely Different Impact of ARRA on Purchases Versus Other Expenditures?

While additional research is needed to form a strong conclusion, one likely explanation for the stark difference in the behavior of state and local purchases and non-purchases in response to ARRA lies in the design of the federal stimulus plan. The lion's share of non-purchase expenditures consists of state and local spending on health and welfare programs; in particular, Medicaid, TANF (Temporary Assistance for Needy Families), and general assistance programs.[5] A large share of the ARRA grants was designed to supplement these programs, especially states' Medicaid programs. In the first quarter of 2009, virtually all (99 percent) of ARRA grants are accounted for by Medicaid. In the 2nd quarter of 2010, Medicaid grants still accounted for much of the ARRA total. The ARRA conditioned states' receipt of federal Medicaid grants on their willingness to not reduce benefits nor restrict eligibility rules. In

---

5. Under Section 5001 of the ARRA (P.L.111-5), to be eligible for additional Medicaid grants state Medicaid programs must maintain eligibility standards and benefits that are not more restrictive than those in effect on July 1, 2008. More restrictive eligibility would preclude a state from receiving the increased Medicaid funds until it had restored eligibility standards, methodologies or procedures to those in effect on July 1, 2008. (https://www.cms.gov/Recovery/Downloads/ARRA_FAQs.pdf)

some states, this also meant undoing benefit reductions or eligibility restrictions that had been implemented in the six months prior to the ARRA's enactment. It is possible that this "hold-harmless" provision, in the face of rising health care costs and recession-induced Medicaid enrollment increases, forced states to reallocate funds that would have otherwise been devoted to state and local purchases to their Medicaid programs.

To examine this hypothesis we split ARRA grants into two components, Medicaid grants and all other ARRA grants, and we then re-estimated the above regressions. In our original research on this project (using data through the second quarter of 2010) we found the effects of Medicaid grants on purchases to be negative and significant. However, when we added new incoming data through the third quarter of 2011, the coefficient turned from negative and significant to positive and insignificant, as Medicaid grants dropped sharply starting in the first quarter of 2011. Hence, splitting the grants into Medicaid versus non-Medicaid does not in the end provide evidence in support of this hypothesis.

## A Counterfactual

What would have happened to government purchases in the counterfactual event that there had not been an ARRA? One way to answer this question is to simulate the estimated equations under the assumption that ARRA grants are zero and that other state and local receipts are unchanged. The resulting impacts on purchases, other expenditures, and net borrowing are shown in Table 7. The first column shows actual ARRA grants and the actual cumulative changes in purchases, other expenditures, and borrowing from their pre-ARRA levels (fourth quarter of 2008). From the first quarter of 2009 to the third quarter of 2011, state and local govern-

**Table 7.** Total changes in budget amounts from pre–ARRA levels: 2009Q1 to 2011Q3 (cumulative change from 2008Q4, billions of dollars).

|  | *Actual* | *Counterfactual* | *Difference* |
|---|---|---|---|
| ARRA Grants | 246 | 0 | −246 |
| Purchases | −19 | 83 | 102 |
| Other Expenditures | 162 | 38 | −124 |
| Net Borrowing | −257 | −33 | 224 |

ments received a total of $246 billion in ARRA grants. During this period, these governments reduced their rate of borrowing compared to pre-ARRA levels by $257 billion, reduced their purchases of goods and services by $19 billion, and increased other expenditures by $162 billion.

In the counterfactual absence of ARRA, the simulations indicate that state and local governments would not have reduced their net borrowing by nearly as much. We show this in the last row of the second column labeled "counterfactual" in Table 7, where net borrowing increases from −$257 billion to −$33 billion, or by $224 billion. The counterfactual increase in "other expenditures" of $38 billion, also shown in Table 7, would have been $124 billion less than the actual increase. And purchases would have risen by $83 billion rather than falling by $19 billion, a difference of $102 billion. Note that this difference in state and local government purchases is larger than the $44 billion increase in federal purchases due to ARRA over the 2009Q1–2011Q3 period as discussed earlier, suggesting that ARRA may have actually reduced total government purchases. (Because the model fits very well, the differences between the actual data and the counterfactual estimates are very close to the differences between simulations with ARRA and the counterfactual simulations without ARRA.)

## Acquiring Financial Assets as ARRA Grants Came In

One objection to this counterfactual hypothesis is that state and local governments would have found it difficult to increase their net borrowing if ARRA had not existed. Because of the financial crisis and their own budget problems, perhaps they were effectively constrained from borrowing more than they actually did, or perhaps interest rates in the capital markets were too high to borrow. However, these governments would not have had to go to the capital markets to increase their net borrowing. They could have increased their net borrowing by drawing down, or at least not increasing, their holdings of financial assets. As a matter of accounting, net borrowing equals the net increase in financial liabilities less the increase in financial assets. An increase in net borrowing occurs when the net acquisition of financial assets is smaller than the net increase in liabilities.

In fact, the Flow of Funds data from the Federal Reserve shows that the counterfactual increase in net borrowing would have been quite likely even if there were borrowing constraints. According to the latest annual data (September 16, 2011), during the first two years of ARRA, from the beginning of 2009 to the end of 2010, net borrowing by state and local governments fell by about $92 billion, while their net increase in liabilities rose by $55 billion and their net acquisition of financial assets rose by $147 billion ($92 = 55 − 147$). Thus, as a whole, state and local governments added substantially to their financial assets as ARRA grants came in. Apparently, they saved much of that new grant money.

For net borrowing to have increased in the counterfactual compared with history, state and local governments could simply have not increased their acquisition of financial assets in the counterfactual by as much as they actually did. Even without increasing their liabilities, the state governments could have increased their net borrowing. Hence, the counterfactual of more net borrowing with ARRA, as in Table 7, seems quite plausible.

## 3. Comparison with Initial Estimates of Government Purchases

The total impact that ARRA has had on government purchases can be obtained by combining federal purchases with state and local purchases. The BEA data on the impact of ARRA on federal purchases from Table 1 show that total increase in federal government purchases from ARRA was between 0.1 and 0.2 percent of GDP during 2009 and 2010. Our counterfactual simulations estimate that state and local government purchases could actually have been smaller as a result of ARRA with a total negative net effect.

The forecasts of economists in and out of government in early 2009 of the likely effect of ARRA on government purchases were much larger than 0.1 to 0.2 percent of GDP, let alone the possible negative effect. Cogan, Cwik, Taylor, and Wieland (2010) assumed that ARRA would raise total government purchases by .47 percent of GDP by the second quarter of 2009 and by .77 percent by the second quarter of 2010 (see the February 2009 working paper version of the published paper). Hall (2009, Table 6), citing the Congressional Budget Office (CBO), assumed that ARRA would raise total government purchases by .49 and .73 percent of GDP in calendar years 2009 and 2010, respectively, which is very close to the assumption used by Cogan, Cwik, Taylor, and Wieland.

In making such predictions, economists analyzing the effect of ARRA assumed that the federal grants to state and local governments would generate a larger increase in purchases than what actually occurred. Romer and Bernstein (2009) assumed in January 2009 that 60 percent of grants would go to purchases, stat-

**Table 8.** Comparison with initial estimates of the multiplicand (change in *G* as a percent of GDP assuming no change at the state and local level).

| | Quarterly | |
| --- | --- | --- |
| | *Initial (CCTW)* | *Actual* |
| 2009Q2 | .47 | .01 |
| 2010Q2 | .77 | .15 |
| | Annual | |
| | *Initial (Hall, CBO)* | *Actual* |
| 2009 | .49 | .05 |
| 2010 | .73 | .15 |

ing that "One dollar of state fiscal relief is assumed to result in $0.60 in higher government purchases." Cogan, Cwik, Taylor, and Wieland (2010) used the same 60 percent conversion factor from grants to purchases. The CBO did not explicitly state a conversion factor from grants to purchases, but the CBO analysis (see March 2009 estimate in Elmendorf (2009)) applied a government purchases multiplier to grants which was the same size as the multiplier applied to federal purchases in the case of infrastructure spending and 70 percent of the federal purchases multiplier in the case of government consumption, implying a grant-to-purchases conversion of between 70 and 100 percent, which is even greater than 60 percent. As stated above, Hall (2009) cites the CBO as a source for the effect of ARRA on government purchases. Table 8 summarizes the differences between these initial estimates and the estimates from this paper assuming that the change in purchases at the federal level are zero rather than negative.

These initial estimates were based largely on guesswork since there are no reliable empirical estimates of how state and local governments respond to the receipt of temporary federal grants. But, by the summer of 2009 it was becoming clear that these initial estimates were far too high; government purchases were not contributing to the recovery as much as the initial estimates predicted. Cogan, Taylor, and Wieland (2009) reported that non-defense government purchases contributed less than 1 percentage point to the 5.4 percentage point real GDP growth improvement from the first to the second quarter of 2009. The low response rate of government purchases to ARRA is likely the principal reason for the difference between the initial estimates of the ARRA's impact and what actually happened.[6]

## 4. Previous Experience with Countercyclical Stimulus Grants to the States

Our results are strikingly similar to those found by Gramlich (1978, 1979) in his influential empirical studies of state and local government finances and in particular the impact of the Carter Administration's 1977 countercyclical stimulus program. The 1977 program attempted to stimulate aggregate economic output by providing federal funds to state and local governments in the form of grants for countercyclical revenue sharing (CRS), local public works projects, and public service employment (PSE).

Using quarterly data from 1954–1977, Gramlich estimated the separate impact of each type of grant on state and local purchases. He found that revenue sharing grants had only a negligible impact on purchases and concluded that "not much of a macro-

---

6. Romer and Bernstein and Cogan, Cwik, Taylor, and Wieland (2010) also assumed a one-quarter lag between the transfer to state and local governments and the increase in purchases by these governments.

stimulation case could be made for CRS." He found that federal grants for public works, by delaying locally-financed projects, actually reduced state and local purchases and thus appeared "to have effects that are perverse." Finally, he found that PSE grants had only a short-run impact that dissipated rapidly with time, "leading to no impact of PSE on total expenditures after four quarters." These findings led Gramlich to conclude "that the general idea of stimulating the economy through state and local governments is probably not a very good one."

## 5. Policy Implications

These empirical findings as well as the similar previous findings of Gramlich (1979) have important implications for the evaluation, design, and feasibility of countercyclical stimulus programs.

First, because in the U.S. federal system, states and localities make decisions about their own government budgets, it is essential to take account of their behavioral responses in assessing the efficacy of federal transfers as a tool for macroeconomic stimulus. As our work and the earlier work of Gramlich (1979) demonstrate, the federal government has only limited ability to affect state and local budget decisions in particular ways, especially over a short period of time when money is fungible and the timing of projects can be postponed or grants can substitute for capital borrowing. The implication is not that the stimulus programs should be even bigger or should be designed better, but rather that such programs are inherently limited by these feasibility constraints.

Second, when assessing the efficacy of providing macroeconomic stimulus transfers to state and local governments, the composition of the transfers matters. We estimate that because the Medicaid grants contained provisions that require state and local governments to maintain benefits and eligibility rules, the grants actually reduced state and local government purchases. The initial evaluation of ARRA failed to account for this and assumed instead that each dollar of grants—whether Medicaid or non-Medicaid—would increase state and local purchases by between 60 cents and a dollar.

Third, when analyzing policy proposals, knowledge gained from prior experiences and from empirical and theoretical studies of those experiences is invaluable. But if the knowledge is discarded or forgotten then it obviously cannot have a constructive influence on analysis or decision making. Preserving this historical knowledge in a readily usable and understandable form for future generations of policy analysts who will face their own economic crises deserves more emphasis in schools, research institutes, and government agencies.

## 6. Conclusion

In this paper we have examined the effect of the American Economic Recovery and Reinvestment Act of 2009 on government purchases of goods and services using new data provided by the Commerce Department. Considering both the federal and the state and local sector, we find the effects of ARRA on government purchases to be remarkably small despite the large overall size of ARRA. It appears that the ARRA grants were allocated to transfer payments, such as Medicaid, and to reducing net borrowing by state and local governments rather than to increasing government purchases. Debates about the size of the government purchases multiplier are thus of less practical importance in the case of ARRA than many may have thought because the multiplicand is so small. Basic economic theory implies that temporary increases in transfer payments have a much smaller impact on GDP than government purchases do. The counterfactual hypothesis that government purchases would have been even worse without ARRA does not seem plausible based on contemporaneous data or historical experience.

These results are quite similar to those of Gramlich (1979) in his studies of comparable countercyclical stimulus programs more than three decades ago. Experience from the 1977 stimulus package and from the 2009 stimulus package shows that grants to state and local governments do not necessarily result in increases in government purchases. The general policy implications are that when evaluating or designing such programs, economists should factor in the reality of past experiences with similar programs and take account of the behavior of state and local governments as well as federal government agencies, recognizing that incentives and disincentives built into the programs affect that behavior.

Our findings are also relevant to a key question: why has the economic recovery been so slow? First, the findings provide a reason why the economic recovery has been slower than the forecasts of many econometric models which had assumed a larger impact of ARRA on purchases. Second, to the extent that the multiplier for government purchases is larger than the multiplier from a temporary increase in transfer payments, the results indicate that ARRA actually reduced aggregate demand and thus delayed the economic recovery from the recession. Third, to the extent that ARRA increased the federal debt—both directly through its deficit financing and indirectly through its de-emphasis on controlling spending—it has likely been a drag on economic growth as concerns about the growing debt increased uncertainty and held back investment in plant and equipment by businesses.

## References

Christiano, Lawrence J., Martin Eichenbaum, Charles L Evans (2005), "Nominal Rigidities and the Dynamic Effects of a Shock to Monetary Policy," *Journal of Political Economy* 113: 1–45.

Christiano, Lawrence, Martin Eichenbaum, and Sergio Rebelo (2011), "When Is the Government Spending Multiplier Large?" *Journal of Political Economy* 119, no. 1: 78–121. Revised version of Northwestern University working paper, August 2009.

Coenen, Guenter, Chris Erceg, Charles Freedman, Davide Furceri, Michael Kumhof, René Lalonde, Douglas Laxton, Jesper Lindé, Annabelle Mourougane, Dirk Muir, Susanna Mursula, Carlos de Resende, John Roberts, Werner Roeger, Stephen Snudden, Mathias Trabandt, Jan in't Veld (2012), "Effects of Fiscal Stimulus in Structural Models," *American Economic Journal: Macroeconomics,* 4(1): 22–68.

Cogan, John F., Tobias Cwik, John B. Taylor, and Volker Wieland (2010), "New Keynesian versus Old Keynesian Government Spending Multipliers," *Journal of Economic Dynamics and Control 34, no. 3*, 281–295. Revised version of Stanford Institute of Economic Policy Research Discussion Paper No. 08–030, February 2009.

Cogan, John F., John B. Taylor, and Volker Wieland (2009), "The Stimulus Didn't Work," *Wall Street Journal,* September 17.

Drautzburg, Thorsten, and Harald Uhlig, (2010), "Fiscal Stimulus and Distortionary Taxation," University of Chicago, January 2010.

Eggertsson, Gauti (2010), "What Fiscal Policy is Effective at Zero Interest Rates," in *Macroeconomics Annual* 25, Daron Acemoglu and Michael Woodford (eds), National Bureau of Economic Research.

Elmendorf, Douglas (2009), Letter to Charles Grassley on the Impact of the American Recovery and Reinvestment Act of 2009, March 2, 2009.

Erceg, Christopher J. and Jesper Linde (2009), "Is There a Fiscal Free Lunch in a Liquidity Trap?" Federal Reserve Board, April 2009.

Gramlich, Edward M. (1978), "State and Local Budgets the Day after it Rained: Why is the Surplus So High?" *Brookings Paper on Economic Activity* 1, 191–216.

Gramlich, Edward M. (1979), "Stimulating the Macro Economy Through

State and Local Governments," *American Economic Review* 69, no. 2, 180–185.

Hall, Robert E. (2009), "By How Much Does GDP Rise If the Government Buys More Output?" *Brookings Papers on Economic Activity 2:* 183–250, also NBER Working Paper No. 15496, November 2009.

Newey, Whitney and Kenneth West (1987), "A Simple Positive Semi-Definite, Heteroskedasticity and Autocorrelation Consistent Covariance Matrix," *Econometrica,* 55, 703–708.

Ramey, Valeria A. (2011), "Can Government Purchases Stimulate the Economy," *Journal of Economic Literature,* 49, no. 3, 673–685.

Romer, Christina and Jared Bernstein (2009), "The Job Impact of the American Recovery and Reinvestment Plan," January 8, 2009.

Smets, Frank and Rafael Wouters (2007), "Shocks and Frictions in U.S. Business Cycles: A Bayesian DSGE Approach," *American Economic Review* 97, 586–606.

Woodford, Michael (2010), "Simple Analytics of the Government Expenditure Multiplier," Columbia University, June 2010.

# CHAPTER 6

# The Great Recession and Delayed Economic Recovery: A Labor Productivity Puzzle?

## ELLEN R. MCGRATTAN AND EDWARD C. PRESCOTT[*]

## Introduction

Prior to the mid-1980s, labor productivity growth was a useful barometer of the U.S. economy's performance: it was low when the economy was depressed and high when it was booming. The correlation between GDP per hour and GDP was over 50 percent between 1960 and 1985. Since then, the correlation between GDP per hour and GDP—both relative to their long-term trends—has been close to zero. Researchers have used the large difference in these correlations as evidence that real business cycle (RBC) theories—theories that assume cyclical fluctuations are driven in large part by shocks to total factor productivity (TFP)—are inconsistent with U.S. data because TFP shocks lead simultaneously to high output per hour and high output. In this paper, we reassess this view and find that eulogies for RBC theories are premature.

[*] We thank Erick Sager for comments on an earlier draft and Joan Gieseke for editorial assistance. The views expressed herein are those of the authors and not necessarily those of the Federal Reserve Bank of Minneapolis or the Federal Reserve System.

Specifically, we reassess recent events of the Great Recession of 2008–2009 and the slow recovery period from 2009–2011 with the version of a real business cycle model used by McGrattan and Prescott (2010) to study the 1990s technology boom.[1] The main difference between this model and earlier vintages of real business cycle models is the inclusion of intangible capital and nonneutral technology change in the production of final goods and services and new intangible capital. McGrattan and Prescott (2010) found that once these additional features of reality are introduced into the RBC model, the theoretical predictions are in close conformity to U.S. observations for 1990–2003, a period which includes a boom period with labor productivity below trend and two depressed periods with labor productivity above trend. Here, we show that these additional features have the potential to also generate the pattern of labor productivity growth observed in the U.S. 2008–2011 period.

Intangible capital is accumulated know-how from investing in research and development, brands, and organizations, which is for the most part expensed by companies rather than capitalized. Because it is expensed, it is not included in measures of business value added and thus is not included in GDP. In a typical downturn, GDP falls but investments fall by more than GDP in percentage terms. By measuring labor productivity as the ratio of GDP to total labor input, one underestimates the fall in total output, which is measured output plus all unmeasured investment, and therefore underestimates the fall in actual labor productivity. In other words, it is possible to observe high measured labor pro-

---

1. The model is an extension of models developed earlier, most notably by Kydland and Prescott (1982) and Hansen (1985).

ductivity while output is low if some output is not included in the statistic but all hours of work are included. The specific pattern of labor productivity over the business cycle depends in large part on the nature of the comovement of relative TFPs in production of final goods and services (that is, GDP) and of new intangible capital.

Using a version of the RBC model with intangible capital and nonneutral technology, we conduct a business cycle accounting exercise in the spirit of Chari, Kehoe, and McGrattan (2007) for the period 2004–2011.[2] First, we show that fluctuations in the sectoral TFPs have the same impact on the business cycle as time-varying efficiency and labor wedges—wedges between marginal rates of substitution and transformation that drive fluctuations in Chari, Kehoe, and McGrattan's prototype growth model. If the model had no intangible capital and changes in TFP were neutral, then conventional wisdom about RBC theory would be right: it predicts that labor productivity is low in depressed periods. Adding intangible capital generates an apparent labor wedge between the marginal rate of substitution between consumption and leisure and *measured* labor productivity. When we add nonneutral technology change, it is possible to generate cyclical behavior in this wedge over the cycle that is consistent with the seemingly puzzling patterns in labor productivity.

---

2. The exercise we conduct here is slightly different from that in McGrattan and Prescott (2010), who studied the technology boom of the 1990s and assumed changes in policies impacting households' intertemporal decisions were inconsequential. In the recent downturn, many argue that the policies impacting households' intertemporal decisions are not inconsequential. Later, we contrast the exercise conducted by McGrattan and Prescott (2010) with what we do in this chapter. See also Ohanian and Raffo (2012), who conduct a cross-country business cycle accounting exercise.

In our business cycle accounting exercise, we feed into the model sectoral TFPs that generate the pattern of GDP and labor productivity that we observed in the United States over the period 2004–2011. In our simulations, we include time-varying taxes on consumption and labor, since these taxes also affect the labor wedge. We abstract from time-varying tax rates on capital and other policies that impact the intertemporal decisions of firms and households, and thus we cannot by construction fit all of the time series of interest. But we ask, How close do we come to generating patterns in consumption, aggregate investment, and business investment that we observe in U.S. data over this period? We find the results are surprisingly close *given that we have abstracted from any financial market or fiscal distortions that might have affected investment returns.*

We then ask, Does the model predict an implausible drop in intangible investment? We find that the model predicts a fall in business intangible investment of the same magnitude as the fall in business tangible investment. We also compare the predicted path for intangible investment to subcomponents that we can measure (e.g., expenditures on R&D and advertising) and to series that move with intangible investments (e.g., the market value of businesses). We find that the patterns and magnitudes of the model predictions are consistent with observations. In essence, we find that the labor productivity puzzle is not a puzzle as previously thought.

As an additional check on the theory, we provide empirical evidence for negative shocks to TFP, which are the main sources of decline in predicted real activity. The evidence we consider are costs paid by businesses to comply with federal regulations and expenditures and employment of federal regulatory agencies. We interpret the increase in regulatory costs as a decrease in TFP. The evidence shows that these costs have risen dramatically in recent years.

The vast literature that attempts to understand the factors giving rise to aggregate fluctuations is too great to survey here. We should note, however, that recent events have spurred a renewed interest in the subject.[3] Most of the papers in this burgeoning literature emphasize the need for new theories, but as far as we know, none has demonstrated large deviations between observations and existing theory.[4]

In the following section, we start with the facts about trends in U.S. labor productivity and discuss the recent comovements of GDP and labor productivity. The subsequent section lays out the theory we use. The next section assesses the recent events in light of this theory. The final section concludes.

## The Facts

The starting point for our study is U.S. labor productivity. As is well known, labor productivity has become less procyclical in the United States.[5] Figures 1 and 2 demonstrate this fact for the aggregate economy and the business sector.

---

3. See, for example, the survey by Ohanian (2010) and recent work exploring the impact of stochastic volatility by Bloom (2009) and Bloom et al. (2011), financial frictions by Arellano, Bai, and Kehoe (2011) and Campello, Graham, and Harvey (2010), labor market distortions by Galí and van Rens (2010), Garin, Pries, and Sims (2011), Mulligan (2011), Schaal (2012), and Berger (2012), monetary policy by Gertler and Kiyotaki (2010), and uncertainty about fiscal policy by McGrattan (forthcoming).

4. Predictions of new theories are typically compared to those of the earlier vintages of RBC models.

5. A useful source for studies on productivity trends is the Bureau of Labor Statistics *Monthly Labor Review*. See, for example, Holman, Joyeux, and Kask (2008) and

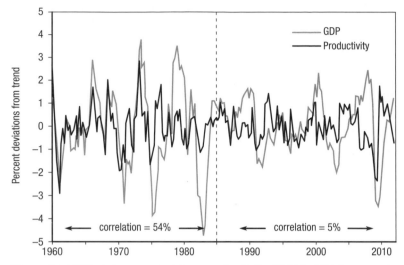

**Figure 1.** GDP and aggregate labor productivity, 1960:1–2011:4, percent deviations from HP-filtered trend.

Figure 1 shows percent deviations of GDP and labor productivity from trend for the aggregate economy during the period 1960:1–2011:4. Labor productivity in this case is the ratio of GDP to total hours of work for the U.S. economy as constructed by Prescott, Ueberfeldt, and Cociuba (2005). The formula for trend is based on Hodrick and Prescott (1997). The correlation for the first half of the sample is 54 percent, and it is obvious from the figure that labor productivity was high in booms and low in depressions. The correlation for the second half is only 5 percent and, unlike the first half, there is no procyclical pattern. During the early 1990s and early 2000s, labor productivity does not decline as much as GDP and recovers faster. By the end of the sample, when

Chernousov, Fleck, and Glaser (2009).

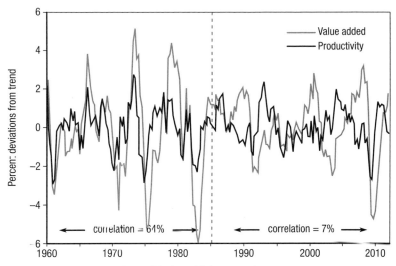

**Figure 2.** Business value added and labor productivity, 1960:1–2011:3, percent deviations from HP-filtered trend.

the depressed period of 2008–2009 is evident, we see that labor productivity is again above its trend while GDP is below.

Figure 2 shows the same statistics, but here we use data for business value added and business hours over the period 1960:1–2011:3. The business sector includes corporate and noncorporate business. In the first half of the sample, the correlation between value added and labor productivity is 64 percent, which is even higher than it is for the overall economy. In the second half, the correlation is only 7 percent, and again the procyclical pattern is no longer evident.

If we zoom in on the end of the sample in either Figure 1 or Figure 2, we see that labor productivity is above trend while outputs, both GDP and business value added, are below trend. This is the puzzle we seek to explore.

We next ask, What does theory tell us about this puzzle?

## Theory

In this section, we lay out the theory we use to study the comovement of output and productivity. We extend the basic framework of the early real business cycle literature by including intangible capital and sectoral TFPs that are nonneutral. In our earlier work, we found that including these additional features eliminated a large deviation from theory that had existed for studying the 1990s technology boom. Here, we find that including these additional features is needed to generate a comovement in labor productivity and GDP that is consistent with U.S. data.

We start by describing the two technologies available to businesses, which are given by

$$y_{bt} = A_t^1 (k_{Tt}^1)^\theta (k_{It})^\phi (h_t^1)^{1-\theta-\phi} \tag{1}$$

$$x_{It} = A_t^2 (k_{Tt}^2)^\theta (k_{It})^\phi (h_t^2)^{1-\theta-\phi} \tag{2}$$

Firms produce business output $y_b$ using their tangible capital $k_T^1$, intangible capital $k_I$, and labor $h^1$. Firms produce new intangible capital $x_I$—such as new brands, new products R&D, patents, etc.—using tangible capital $k_T^2$, intangible capital $k_I$, and labor $h^2$. The total stock of intangible capital $k_I$ is an input to both business sectors; it is not split between them, as is the case for tangible capital and labor. The idea is that intangibles such as brands and patents are used both to sell final goods and services and by designers and researchers developing new intangible capital.

Given $(k_{T0}, k_{I0})$, the stand-in household maximizes

$$E \sum_{t=0}^{\infty} \beta^t [\log c_t + \psi \log(1 - h_t)] N_t \tag{3}$$

subject to

$$c_t + x_{Tt} + q_t x_{It} = r_{Tt} k_{Tt} + r_{It} k_{It} + w_t h_t + \zeta_t$$

$$- \tau_{ct} c_t - \tau_{ht}(w_t h_t - (1-\chi)q_t x_{It}) - \tau_k k_{Tt}$$

$$- \tau_p \{ r_{Tt} k_{Tt} + r_{It} k_{It} - \delta_T k_{Tt} - \chi q_t x_{It} - \tau_k k_{Tt} \}$$

$$- \tau_d \{ r_{Tt} k_{Tt} + r_{It} k_{It} - x_{Tt} - \chi q_t x_{It} - \tau_k k_{Tt}$$

$$- \tau_p (r_{Tt} k_{Tt} + r_{It} k_{It} - \delta_T k_{It} - \chi q_t x_{It} - \tau_k k_{Tt}) \} \quad (4)$$

$$k_{T,t+1} = [(1-\delta_T)k_{Tt} + x_{Tt}]/(1+\eta) \tag{5}$$

$$k_{I,t+1} = [(1-\delta_I)k_{It} + x_{It}]/(1+\eta). \tag{6}$$

All variables in equations (3)–(6) are written in per capita terms, and $N_t = N_0(1+\eta)^t$ is the population in $t$. Households discount future utility at rate $\beta$. Consumption $c$ includes both private and public consumption, and investment $x_T$ includes both private and public tangible investment. The relative price of intangible investment $x_I$ and consumption is $q$. The rental rates for business tangible and intangible capital are denoted by $r_T$ and $r_I$, respectively, and the wage rate for labor is denoted by $w$. Inputs are paid their marginal products. Capital depreciates at rates $\delta_T$ and $\delta_I$ for tangible and intangible capital, respectively. Other income is denoted by $\zeta$, and the remaining terms in the household budget constraint are tax payments.

Taxes are levied on consumption at rate $\tau_c$, labor income at rate $\tau_h$, tangible capital (that is, property) at rate $\tau_k$, profits at rate $\tau_p$, and capital distributions at rate $\tau_d$. Note that taxable income for the tax on profits is net of depreciation and property tax, and taxable income for the tax on distributions is net of property tax and profits tax. Note also that we have assumed varying tax rates only for consumption and labor. These rates directly impact the wedge between marginal rates of substitution and labor productivity and can be easily measured.[6] We have abstracted from any variation in capital taxes—or expectations in changes in capital taxes—because we want to see how much of a deviation between theory and data there is if we include only shocks to efficiency and labor wedges.

Other income $\zeta$ is exogenous in the household's decision problem and includes government transfers and nonbusiness capital income net of taxes and investment. Nonbusiness labor income is included in $wh$. We treat hours, investment, and output in the nonbusiness sector exogenously—denoting them with an overbar—because this sector is not important for the issues being addressed. To be precise, in our simulations of the model, we set the paths of nonbusiness hours $\{\bar{h}_{nt}\}$, investment $\{\bar{x}_{nt}\}$, and output $\{\bar{y}_{nt}\}$ in the model's nonbusiness sector equal to U.S. paths. Measured output, which corresponds to GDP, is the sum of $y_b$ and $\bar{y}_n$. Measured tangible investment is the sum of business tangible investment $x_T$ and nonbusiness tangible investment $\bar{x}_n$. Measured hours $h$ is the sum of business hours $h^1 + h^2$ and nonbusiness hours $\bar{h}_n$.

The parameter $\chi$ represents the fraction of intangible investment financed by capital owners. The amount $\chi q x_I$ is expensed investment, which is financed by the capital owners who have lower accounting profits the greater this type of investment. The

---

6. Braun (1994) and McGrattan (1994) extended early real business cycle models that predicted too little variation in hours to include variations in tax rates that have a first-order effect on hours of work.

amount $(1-\chi)qx_I$ is what McGrattan and Prescott (2010) call *sweat investment*, which is financed by workers who have lower compensation the greater this type of investment. These investments are made with the expectation of future capital gains when the business is sold or goes public.

Gross domestic product in the economy is the sum of total consumption (public plus private) and tangible investment (public plus private) for business and nonbusiness; in per capita terms GDP is $c + x_T \mid \bar{x}_n$. Gross domestic income (GDI) is the sum of all labor income less sweat investment, $wh - (1-\chi)qx_I$, business capital income less expensed investment, $r_T k_T + r_I k_I - \chi qx_I$, and nonbusiness capital income (which is found residually as the difference between GDP and the other components of GDI). Summing terms gives us GDI equal to $y_b + \bar{y}_n$. Total output and income—which is not what is measured by national accountants—includes the value of intangible capital and is therefore equal to GDP (or GDI) plus $qx_I$.

## A Possible Resolution of the Puzzle

Next we show that the model has the potential to resolve the labor productivity puzzle. To gain intuition for why, it helps to first consider the simplest one-sector growth model ($\phi = 0$) that abstracts from any fiscal policies or nonbusiness activity, which is the prototype model used by Chari, Kehoe, and McGrattan (2007). In that model, the production technology is given by $y_t = A_t k_t^{\theta} h_t^{1-\theta}$, where $y$ is total output, $A$ is aggregate TFP, $k$ is total tangible capital, and $h$ is total hours. On impact, with the capital stock given, a shock to TFP has a direct effect on output through $A$ and an indirect effect through hours $h$. If the shock is negative, the fall in output has to exceed the fall in hours and therefore labor productivity $y/h$ falls.

When we introduce intangible capital and nonneutral TFP (that is, $A_t^1$ not necessarily changing by the same factor as $A_t^2$), we find that the positive correlation between output and labor productivity is not guaranteed. There are two reasons for this result. First, measured output of the business sector in equation (1) does not depend on total business hours $h^1+h^2$, only on business hours allocated to the production of final goods and services. Second, true output of the business sector is $y_b+qx_I$, not $y_b$. Therefore, there is a difference between measured labor productivity and true labor productivity.

For the aggregate economy, measured labor productivity is the ratio of GDP, $y_b+y_n$, to total hours, $h$, while true labor productivity is the ratio of total output, $y_b+y_n+qx_I$, to total hours, $h$. For the business sector, measured labor productivity is the ratio of business value added, $y_b$, to total business hours, $h^1+h^2$, while true labor productivity is the ratio of total business output, $y_b+qx_I$, to total business hours, $h^1+h^2$ (or, equivalently, the ratio of output of final goods and services in the business sector, $y_b$, to total hours allocated to production of final goods and services, $h^1$).

What does this imply for the labor productivity puzzle? If shocks to the sectoral TFPs move in opposite directions or change at different rates, the model predicts a shift in hours from one activity to another. Suppose, for example, that true output in the business sector, $y_b+qx_I$, and true labor productivity, $(y_b+qx_I)/(h^1+h^2)$, both fall in a downturn. What that means for *measured* labor productivity depends on the change in $qx_I$ relative to output $y_b$. If investment falls by more than output, which is typical in depressed periods, then it is possible that measured labor productivity would rise.

Variations in $qx_I$ act like a time-varying labor wedge, as can be seen by households' intratemporal first-order condition

$$\psi(1+\tau_{ct})\frac{c_t}{1-h_t} = (1-\tau_{ht})(1-\theta-\phi)\frac{y_{bt}+qx_{It}}{h_t^1+h_t^2}, \tag{7}$$

which relates the marginal rate of substitution between consumption and leisure to the after-tax marginal product of labor. Notice that the right-hand side of equation (7) is a function of true labor productivity, not measured labor productivity. If business value added or GDP is used as the output measure when constructing the wedge, it will be a function not only of the tax rates but also of the value of intangible capital. The same will be true if we compare the marginal rate of substitution to *measured* compensation per hour. In other words, there is an apparent wedge between the marginal rate of substitution and the wage rate of workers.[7]

## Identifying Total Factor Productivities

In McGrattan and Prescott (2010), when deriving estimates of sectoral TFPs, we used the fact that there was little change in policies impacting households' *intertemporal* decisions during the 1990s (e.g., policies related to capital taxation or financial markets). That allowed us to use intertemporal first-order conditions of households to derive estimates of sectoral TFPs. More specifically, we

---

7. If the wedge were instead between the wage rate and the marginal product of labor, then we would not have a resolution to the labor productivity puzzle because the time series of U.S. compensation per hour and U.S. GDP per hour are close.

used one of the intertemporal conditions to obtain the relative price of intangible and tangible investment.[8]

For 2008–2009, it is hard to make the case a priori that the changes in financial markets and fiscal policies were inconsequential. Therefore, we do a different kind of exercise here, more in the spirit of business cycle accounting (see Chari, Kehoe, and McGrattan 2007). We choose equilibrium paths for sectoral TFPs that imply model predictions for GDP and labor productivity in line with the U.S. analogues. Above we showed that such an exercise is possible once we add intangible capital and nonneutral technology. Of course, it could be the case that deviations from theory still arise or that intangible investments have to be nonsensical to get the large declines in GDP and hours of work that we observed. In this case, we would agree with the conventional wisdom that says RBC theories are missing something important. If, on the other hand, we find that the deviations from theory are small and the implied intangible investments are consistent with available evidence, then the theory will have passed an important test.

## Facts in Light of Theory

In this section, we report the results of our accounting exercise. We first describe the model's benchmark parameterization and exogenous inputs. Then we simulate the model and compare the predicted equilibrium paths to U.S. time series. We find that the model does surprisingly well along many dimensions, including those it was not set up to match.

---

8. See McGrattan and Prescott (2010) for details.

**Table 1.** Model Parameters

| Parameter | Expression | Value |
|---|---|---|
| **Growth Rates** | | |
| Growth in population | $\eta$ | 0.010 |
| Growth in technology | $\gamma$ | 0.019 |
| **Preferences** | | |
| Discount factor | $\beta$ | 0.979 |
| Utility parameter | $\psi$ | 1.186 |
| **Depreciation Rates** | | |
| Tangible capital | $\delta_T$ | 0.039 |
| Intangible capital | $\delta_I$ | 0.039 |
| **Capital Tax Rates** | | |
| Tax rate on property | $\tau_k$ | 0.014 |
| Tax rate on profits | $\tau_p$ | 0.286 |
| Tax rate on distributions | $\tau_d$ | 0.078 |
| **Capital Shares** | | |
| Tangible capital | $\theta$ | 0.212 |
| Intangible capital | $\phi$ | 0.150 |
| **Fraction of intangible capital financed by workers** | $\chi$ | 0.500 |

## Model Inputs

In Tables 1 and 2, we report the model inputs for our simulations. Overall, with the parameters in Table 1 and the 2004 values of exogenous parameters in Table 2, the model's national accounts for 2004 line up with the 2004 U.S. national accounts described in the appendix. More specifically, the growth rates shown in Table 1 are consistent with trend U.S. growth rates. Preference parameters are consistent with U.S. returns to capital and fraction of time in work. Depreciation rates—which are assumed to be equal for

**Table 2.** Time Series for Exogenous Inputs

| $t$ | Tax Rates | | TFP Parameters | | Nonbusiness Series | | |
|---|---|---|---|---|---|---|---|
| | $\tau_{ct}$ | $\tau_{ht}$ | $A^1_t$ | $A^2_t$ | $\bar{y}_{nt}$ | $\bar{x}_{nt}$ | $\bar{h}_{nt}$ |
| 2004 | 6.20 | 35.8 | 1.67 | 1.25 | 0.324 | 0.116 | 0.044 |
| 2005 | 6.35 | 35.1 | 1.67 | 1.18 | 0.316 | 0.113 | 0.046 |
| 2006 | 6.36 | 35.3 | 1.68 | 1.20 | 0.304 | 0.107 | 0.046 |
| 2007 | 6.19 | 35.2 | 1.66 | 1.26 | 0.319 | 0.101 | 0.047 |
| 2008 | 6.00 | 35.2 | 1.63 | 1.25 | 0.323 | 0.086 | 0.048 |
| 2009 | 5.77 | 35.1 | 1.52 | 1.12 | 0.324 | 0.092 | 0.047 |
| 2010 | 5.81 | 35.1 | 1.53 | 1.05 | 0.311 | 0.084 | 0.048 |
| 2011 | 5.95 | 35.1 | 1.54 | 1.07 | 0.301 | 0.079 | 0.047 |

intangible and tangible investment—generate a tangible investment to capital ratio that is consistent with the U.S ratio.[9] Capital tax rates are consistent with taxes on imports and production and income tax policies. Capital shares and the fraction of intangible capital financed by workers are consistent with the breakdown of U.S. national incomes. (See the appendix for more details.)

The construction of the tax rates and nonbusiness series shown in Table 2 are also described in detail in the appendix. The TFP parameters are, as noted earlier, chosen to obtain the right patterns of GDP and aggregate labor productivity. Notice that the TFP parameter for the production of final goods and services, $A^1_t$, falls about 9 percent between 2004 and 2009 and remains low. The TFP parameter for production of new intangible capital, $A^2_t$, falls about 10 percent over the period 2004–2009, but the pattern is different

9. It is not possible to separately identify the depreciation rate and capital share for intangible capital. McGrattan and Prescott (2010) show that what matters is not the specific parameter values but rather the implied intangible capital stock.

from $A_t^1$. It falls initially by 6 percent and then gradually increases before falling again in 2008.

We feed the inputs from Table 2 into the model. In doing so, we assume that households have perfect foresight expectations starting in 2007. Prior to that, they do not anticipate the Great Recession but assume that the current exogenous inputs will persist.[10]

## Model Predictions

The main results are shown in Figures 3–10, which are comparisons of model predictions with U.S. data. The same detrending procedures are used for the model and the data. Specifically, all time series, with the exception of hours, are in real per capita terms and divided by $1.019^t$ to account for growth in technology. Hours are per capita.

Figure 3 shows actual and predicted GDP, which by construction line up nicely. Figure 4 shows per capita hours of work in the aggregate economy, which also lines up nicely. Figure 5 shows the ratio and, as we noted earlier, the fact that labor productivity was increasing between 2008 and 2010 while GDP was falling. In Figure 6, we show the labor productivity for the business sector, which rises sharply between 2009 and 2010.

Figures 7 and 8 show predicted and U.S. total (tangible) investment and consumption—two series that were not matched when choosing sectoral TFPs. Interestingly, we *overpredict* the decline in total tangible investment, which is below trend by about 25 percent

---

10. The assumption of perfect foresight expectations is not critical because there are no intertemporal shocks. In the case of the latter, the modeling of uncertainty is critical. See, for example, McGrattan (forthcoming).

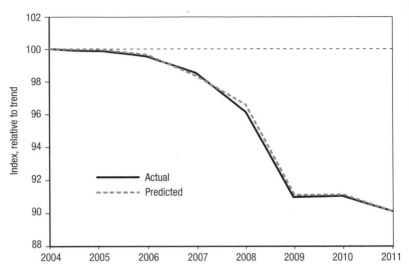

**Figure 3.** Predicted and U.S. real per capita GDP, 2004–2011, relative to a 1.9% trend.

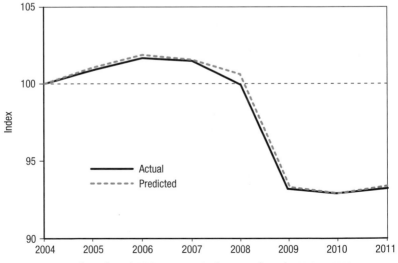

**Figure 4.** Predicted and U.S. per capita hours of work, 2004–2011.

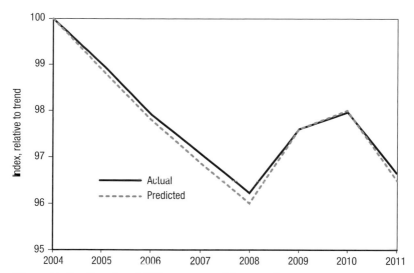

**Figure 5.** Predicted and U.S. aggregate labor productivity, 2004–2011, relative to a 1.9% trend.

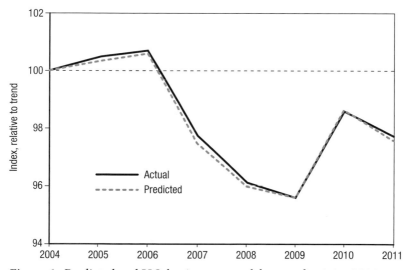

**Figure 6.** Predicted and U.S. business sector labor productivity, 2004–2011, relative to a 1.9% trend.

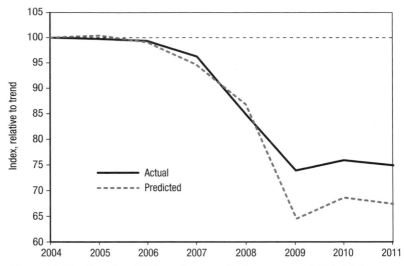

**Figure 7.** Predicted and U.S. real per capita investment, 2004–2011, relative to a 1.9% trend.

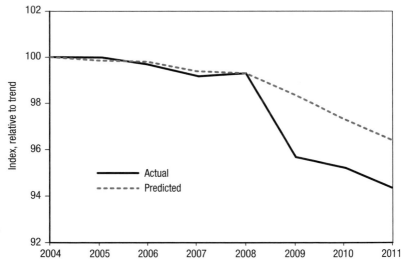

**Figure 8.** Predicted and U.S. real per capita consumption, 2004–2011, relative to a 1.9% trend.

in 2011 for the United States, whereas the model predicts that it is below by 33 percent. This result is somewhat surprising, given that we have abstracted from any credit market or financial market problems associated with the financial crisis. The flip side of the overprediction of the fall in investment is, of course, an underprediction of the fall in consumption, since they sum to GDP.

In Figure 9, we compare the path for model GDP—which is nearly the same as the path for U.S. GDP—and the path for model total output. Total output falls by more in the Great Recession because intangible investment falls by more than the value added of final goods and services. In Figure 10, we compare model predictions of tangible and intangible investments in the business sector. Both investments fall by 50 percent before starting to recover, although the patterns are different. In 2008, intangible investment is roughly 15 percent above trend while tangible investment is on

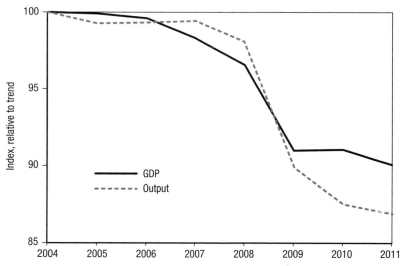

**Figure 9.** Predicted real per capita GDP and total output, 2004–2011, relative to a 1.9% trend.

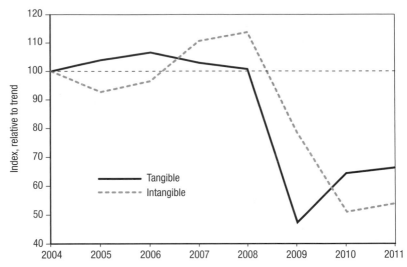

**Figure 10.** Predicted real per capita business investments, 2004–2011, relative to a 1.9% trend.

its trend, and the fall in tangible investment is more abrupt than for intangible investment.

## Evidence of Low Intangible Investment

We next ask if there is any evidence for a rise in intangible investment over the period 2004–2008, as we see in the model predictions, and if there is any evidence of a decline after 2008. Although we do not have comprehensive measures of total intangible investments, we do have some direct measures of industry R&D and advertising expenditures.[11]

---

11. There has been some work done, most notably by Corrado, Hulten, and Sichel (2005, 2006) and Hulten (2010), to estimate other components of intangible investments such as organizational capital and marketing capital, but these authors admit that there is still a lot of guesswork involved.

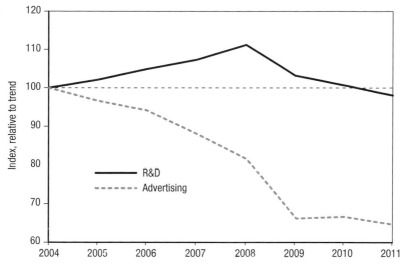

**Figure 11.** U.S. real per capita R&D and advertising expenditures, 2004–2011, relative to a 1.9% trend.

In Figure 11, we plot real per capita R&D expenditures financed and performed by industry and real per capita U.S. advertising expenditures. (See the appendix for details on sources for these data.) We do see a significant rise in R&D expenditures before 2008, although a partial explanation for this result is that the trend growth in R&D over the post–World War II period outpaced GDP growth by about 3 percent per year. In 2008, the trend in R&D is reversed, and relative to its long-run trend, this expenditure series is down close to 20 percent. For advertising, we see a steady decline in expenditures, with the magnitude of the decline about 35 percent by 2009. The percentage decline in U.S. tangible investment lies between 20 and 30 percent and thus adds support for the model that predicts tangible and intangible investment should have fallen by similar magnitudes.

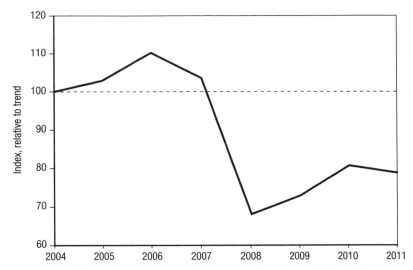

**Figure 12.** U.S. real per capita market value of business, 2004–2011, relative to a 1.9% trend.

Other evidence that supports a significant decline in U.S. intangible investments is found in the market value of businesses. In Figure 12, we plot real per capita market value relative to a 1.9 percent trend. In theory, the market value of businesses is the value of their productive capital stocks, both tangible and intangible. The fall in market values is large: roughly 20 to 30 percent over the sample—a magnitude that is far too large to be attributable solely to a decline in the tangible capital stock of U.S. businesses.

## Evidence of Low TFP

The driving forces of the model are shocks to TFP. Is there any evidence of negative shocks during the recent downturn? In this section, we show that there is direct evidence in higher annual costs of firms for compliance with federal regulations, rising expenditures of federal regulatory agencies, and rising employment of federal regulatory agencies. We interpret higher regulatory costs to businesses as a key factor for lower TFP.

Crain and Crain (2010) estimate that the total costs of federal regulations have increased since 2005 with the cost for 2008 at roughly $8,086 per employee. For firms with fewer than 20 employees, they estimate the cost is $10,585 per employee, which is high when compared to annual wage compensation paid per employee. Crain and Crain estimate costs on those who are regulated and define them to be "resource costs over and above those that show up in the federal budget and agency personnel charts" (p. 12). For example, for pollution control, they include costs of businesses to install abatement equipment, but they do not include spending of the Environmental Protection Agency.

Most predictions for future costs are even higher because the current estimates do not include costs related to the Dodd-Frank legislation for financial firms and President Obama's health care initiatives. In their review of "over-regulated America," the *Economist* noted that the Dodd-Frank law, at 848 pages, is 23 times longer than the Glass-Steagall Act. Although high, that estimate does not take into account that many sections call for further detail to be worked out by the regulators. Mathews (2011), in reporting on new health mandates, points out that the number of codes used to classify an illness or injury will rise from 18,000 to 140,000.[12]

Next consider the spending of federal agencies that regulate households and businesses. In Figure 13, we plot real per capita

---

12. To give an example, in the new system, there are three categories related to drowning and submersion due to falling or jumping from burning water skis.

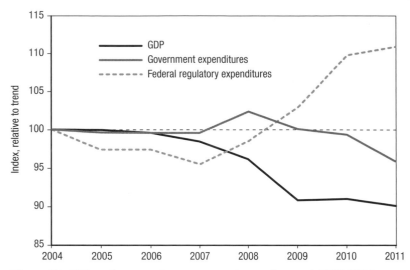

**Figure 13.** U.S. real per capita government spending and GDP, 2004–2011, relative to a 1.9% trend.

government expenditures—both total spending and spending on federal regulatory activities—relative to a 1.9 percent growth trend for 2004–2011. The estimates of regulatory spending are taken from Dudley and Warren (2010) and are based on various issues of the *Budget of the United States Government.* (See the appendix for more details.) For ease of comparison, we plot these expenditures alongside detrended real U.S. GDP for the same period. What we see is that spending on regulatory activities grew significantly faster than total spending and GDP. By 2011, regulatory spending is 11 percent above trend, while GDP is 10 percent below trend.

The picture is even more striking if we use employment instead of spending. In Figure 14, we plot full-time equivalent (FTE) employment for the U.S. economy, the total government sector, and federal regulatory activities for the period 2004–2011.

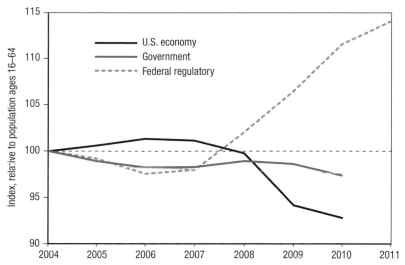

**Figure 14.** Full-time equivalent employment relative to population ages 16–64, 2004–2011.

The source of employment data for the aggregates is the Bureau of Economic Analysis (BEA), and the source of the federal regulatory employment is Dudley and Warren (2010). Each employment series is divided by the population age 16 to 64. By the end of the sample, the number of FTEs in regulatory activities relative to the population is close to 15 percent above its 2004 level. In contrast, the ratio of FTEs to population in the government sector is below trend, and in the overall economy, the ratio is well below trend.

To summarize, we find that a relatively simple RBC theory does surprisingly well in accounting for the recent downturn. Thus far, we have found no macro or microevidence to rule out this theory. In fact, RBC theories look like a good starting point for analyzing the impact of other factors that we abstracted from.

## Conclusion

In this paper, we analyzed the recent Great Recession of 2008–2009 and the slow recovery of 2009–2011 with an RBC model and found that the labor productivity puzzle is not a puzzle as previously thought. The addition of intangible capital and nonneutral technology to the model was crucial in accounting for high productivity and low GDP during the period.

Although we abstracted from many factors that may have played a role during this period, we did not find large deviations from theory. In our view, deviations from theory direct the development of science. Researchers should be aware of what they are jettisoning when moving on to new theories of the business cycle, and policymakers should be cautious of doing more harm than good with quick policy fixes based on untested theories.[13]

## Appendix: Data Sources

The four main sources for our data are the Bureau of Economic Analysis (BEA), which publishes the national accounts and fixed asset tables; the Federal Reserve Board, which publishes the Flow of Funds tables; the Bureau of Labor Statistics, which publishes data on hours and population; and the National Science Foundation (NSF), which publishes statistics on research and development. We also use several auxiliary sources for data on tax rates and intangible expenditures. In this appendix, we provide details on the specific data we use and the necessary revisions we make to the national accounts so that the data are consistent with growth theory.

---

13. For an interesting discussion of the laundry list of policy interventions over the period 2007–2010, see Taylor (2011).

## National Accounts and Fixed Assets

### *Overview and Sources*

Table A (pp. 144–46) contains a summary of the revised national accounts along with values for 2004, all relative to an adjusted measure of GDP that is consistent with theory. The table numbers and sources of the raw data are listed in parentheses. The sources are tables from the BEA's national income and product accounts (NIPA) and fixed asset (FA) tables, and the Federal Reserve's Flow of Funds accounts (FOF). For example, NIPA 1.1.5 is Table 1.1.5 from the BEA NIPA tables. The values shown in the right-hand column of the table are the shares relative to adjusted GDP for 2004. When we compare model predictions with data, we work with real measures and deflate all nominal U.S. time series by the NIPA GDP implicit price deflator.

We have organized Table A as follows. Tables A1 and A2 are the income side of our revised accounts. In Table A1, we display the components of our measure of domestic business value added. This measure is close to the sum of the value added of corporate business, sole proprietorships and partnerships, and other private business as defined in the NIPA tables. In Table A2, we display the components of our measure of domestic nonbusiness value added. This measure is the sum of value added of the household business sector, nonprofits, general government, and government enterprises. Table A3 provides details of the product side of the accounts along with totals for the income side (for comparison). We have categorized tangible investment into business and nonbusiness as in the case of incomes. That is, investments of corporations and noncorporate business are included with business investment, and investments of household business, nonprofits, and government are included with nonbusiness investment.

**Table A.** Revised National Accounts, Relative to Adjusted GDP, 2004

*A1. Domestic Business Value Added*

| | | |
|---|---|---|
| 1 | **Domestic Business Value Added** | .676 |
| 2 | Consumption of fixed capital | .078 |
| 3 |    Corporate business (NIPA 7.5) | .065 |
| 4 |    Sole proprietorships and partnerships (NIPA 7.5) | .011 |
| 5 |    Other private business (NIPA 7.5) | .002 |
| 6 | Labor income | .445 |
| 7 |    Compensation of employees | .388 |
| 8 |      Corporate business (NIPA 1.13) | .340 |
| 9 |      Sole proprietorships and partnerships (NIPA 1.13) | .045 |
| 10 |      Other private business (NIPA 1.13) | .003 |
| 11 |    70% proprietors' income with IVA and CCadj (NIPA 1.13) | .058 |
| 12 | Capital income | .152 |
| 13 |    Corporate profits with IVA and CCadj (NIPA 1.13) | .083 |
| 14 |    30% proprietors' income with IVA and CCadj (NIPA 1.13) | .025 |
| 15 |    Rental income of persons with CCadj (NIPA 1.13) | .004 |
| 16 |    Net interest and miscellaneous payments | .015 |
| 17 |      Corporate business (NIPA 1.13) | .004 |
| 18 |      Sole proprietorships and partnerships (NIPA 1.13) | .008 |
| 19 |      Other private business (NIPA 1.13) | .003 |
| 20 |    Taxes on production and imports[a] | .025 |
| 21 |      Corporate business (NIPA 1.13) | .049 |
| 22 |      Sole proprietorships and partnerships (NIPA 1.13) | .012 |
| 23 |      Other private business (NIPA 1.13) | .001 |
| 24 |    *Less:* Sales tax (NIPA 3.5) | .037 |

*A2. Domestic Nonbusiness Value Added*

| | | |
|---|---|---|
| 1 | **Domestic Nonbusiness Value Added** | .326 |
| 2 | Consumption of fixed capital | .097 |
| 3 |    Households | .073 |
| 4 |      Excluding consumer durables (NIPA 7.5) | .013 |
| 5 |      Consumer durable depreciation (FOF F10) | .060 |

**Table A.**  Revised National Accounts (*continued*)

*A2. Domestic Nonbusiness Value Added*

| | | |
|---|---|---|
| 6 | Nonprofits (NIPA 7.5) | .005 |
| 7 | General government (NIPA 7.5) | .015 |
| 8 | Government enterprises (NIPA 7.5) | .003 |
| 9 | Labor income | .147 |
| 10 | Compensation of employees | .147 |
| 11 | Households (NIPA 1.13) | .001 |
| 12 | Nonprofits (NIPA 1.13) | .043 |
| 13 | General government (NIPA 1.13) | .093 |
| 14 | Government enterprises (NIPA 1.13) | .010 |
| 15 | Capital income | .082 |
| 16 | Current surplus of government enterprises (NIPA 1.13) | .000 |
| 17 | Rental income of persons with CCadj (NIPA 1.13) | .011 |
| 18 | Net interest and miscellaneous payments | .031 |
| 19 | Households (NIPA 1.13) | .030 |
| 20 | Nonprofits (NIPA 1.13) | .001 |
| 21 | Taxes on production and imports[a] | .004 |
| 22 | Households (NIPA 1.13) | .009 |
| 23 | Nonprofits (NIPA 1.13) | .001 |
| 24 | *Less:* Sales tax (NIPA 3.5) | .006 |
| 25 | Imputed additional capital services[b] | .036 |
| 26 | Household, consumer durables | .013 |
| 27 | Government capital | .024 |

*A3. Domestic Value Added and Product*

| | | |
|---|---|---|
| 1 | **Total Adjusted Domestic Income** | 1.000 |
| 2 | **Domestic Business Value Added** | .676 |
| 3 | **Domestic Nonbusiness Value Added** | .326 |
| 4 | **Statistical Discrepancy** | −.002 |
| 5 | **Total Adjusted Domestic Product** | 1.000 |
| 6 | Consumption | .781 |
| 7 | Personal consumption expenditures (NIPA 1.1.5) | .661 |
| 8 | *Less:* Consumer durables (NIPA 1.1.5) | .086 |

**Table A.** Revised National Accounts (*continued*)

*A3. Domestic Value Added and Product*

| | | |
|---|---|---|
| 9 | *Less:* Sales tax, nondurables and services (NIPA 3.5) | .038 |
| 10 | Consumer durable depreciation (FOF F10) | .060 |
| 11 | Government consumption expenditures (NIPA 3.1) | .148 |
| 12 | Imputed additional capital services[b] | .036 |
| 13 | Business tangible investment[c] | .102 |
| 14 | Corporate gross private domestic investment (FOF F6) | .081 |
| 15 | Noncorporate gross private domestic investment (FOF F6) | .021 |
| 16 | Nonbusiness tangible investment | .117 |
| 17 | Household | .128 |
| 18 | Excluding consumer durables (FOF F6) | .047 |
| 19 | Consumer durables (NIPA 1.1.5) | .086 |
| 20 | *Less:* Sales tax, durables (NIPA 3.5) | .005 |
| 21 | Nonprofits (FOF F6) | .008 |
| 22 | Government investment (NIPA 3.1) | .030 |
| 23 | Net exports of goods and services (NIPA 1.1.5) | −.049 |

*Note:* IVA, inventory valuation adjustment; CCadj, capital consumption adjustment.

[a] This category includes business transfers and excludes subsidies.

[b] Imputed additional capital services are equal to 4.1 percent times the current-cost net stock of government fixed assets and consumer durables goods (FA 1.1).

[c] 10 percent of farm business is in corporate, with the remainder in noncorporate.

Data on capital stocks are used to impute some services of capital when we revise the accounts. They are also used to set certain model parameters and to initialize stocks when computing model equilibria. We use BEA reproducible stocks (FA Table 1.1 for totals and FA Table 6.1 by owner). To that we add land values based on Federal Reserve market values of real estate from balance sheets of households (FOF B100), nonfarm nonfinancial corporations (FOF B102), and nonfarm noncorporate (FOF B103).

## Revisions

We now describe two adjustments to GDP and GDI that ensure the national accounts are consistent with our model. They are adjustments for consumption taxes and fixed asset expenditures.

Unlike the NIPA, our model output does not include consumption taxes as part of consumption and as part of value added. We thus subtract sales and excise taxes from the NIPA data on taxes on production and imports (line 24, Table A1 and line 24, Table A2) and from personal consumption expenditures (line 9, Table A3 and line 20, Table A3), since these taxes primarily affect consumption expenditures. As a result of this adjustment, we use producer prices rather than a mixture of producer and consumer prices.

We treat expenditures on all fixed assets as investment. Thus, spending on consumer durables is treated as an investment rather than as a consumption expenditure and moved from private consumption (line 8, Table A3) to nonbusiness tangible investment (line 19, Table A3). We introduce a consumer durables services sector in much the same way as the NIPA introduces owner-occupied housing services. Households rent the consumer durables to themselves. Specifically, we add depreciation of consumer durables to consumption of fixed capital of households (line 5, Table A2) and to private consumption (line 10, Table A3). We add imputed additional capital services for consumer durables to capital income (line 26, Table A2) and to private consumption (line 12, Table A3). We assume a rate of return equal to 4.1 percent, which is an estimate of the return on other types of capital. A related adjustment is made for government capital. Specifically, we add imputed additional capital services for government capital to capital income (line 27, Table A3) and to public consumption (line 12, Table A3).

After the above adjustments are made to the nominal U.S. series, we detrend them by dividing by three factors: (1) the NIPA GDP implicit price deflator; (2) the population series (defined below); and (3) the factor $1.019^t$ to account for growth in technology.

## Hours and Population

The primary source of our hours and population data is the U.S. Department of Labor, Bureau of Labor Statistics, *Employment and Earnings*. The data are based on the Current Population Survey (CPS), and we briefly describe them here. Full details are given in Prescott, Ueberfeldt, and Cociuba (2005).

The population covered by our series is the total noninstitutional population, ages 16 to 64, for the United States. Prior to 1982, military hours are estimated and added to civilian hours from the CPS. After 1982, they are included in the CPS estimate of total hours.

To construct our time series of business hours, we use the BLS index of business hours (PRS84006033) multiplied by an estimate of the fraction of persons at work who are in the business sector for one year (2005) in the CPS survey. Hours in the nonbusiness sector are found by subtracting business hours from the total.

## Tax Rates

We use data from the U.S. national accounts to construct estimates for the tax rate on consumption in Table 2. The tax rate is found by taking the ratio of sales taxes in NIPA to consumption expenditures in NIPA (which include sales taxes). In our measure of sales taxes, we include federal excise taxes and customs, state and local sales taxes, and other nonproperty licenses and fees. Our measure of NIPA consumption expenditures includes adjustments for consumer durables. Denoting sales tax by $\tau_c c$ and NIPA consumption expenditures by $c + \tau_c c$, the ratio yields $\tau_c/(1 + \tau_c)$. It is easy to determine $\tau_c$ from this ratio.

For the marginal tax rate on labor in Table 2, we use Barro and Redlick (2011) and data from the TAXSIM website at the National Bureau of Economic Research (NBER) to extend their series past 2006.

Next, consider the capital tax rates listed in Table 1. The estimate of the tax rate on property is based on NIPA taxes on imports and production. We take property taxes paid by businesses and divide by the total tangible capital stock of businesses. The tax rate on profits is corporate income tax liabilities divided by before-tax profits. Since Federal Reserve banks pay a 100 percent corporate income tax, we subtract their profits from tax liabilities and profits before constructing the ratio. The tax rate on distributions is the average marginal tax rate on dividend income constructed from individual income tax data. The rate takes into account that pension funds, IRAs, and nonprofits pay a tax rate of zero. See McGrattan (forthcoming) for more details on constructing the tax rate on distributions.

## Intangible Expenditures and Market Values

The source of R&D expenditures shown in Figure 11 is the National Science Foundation (2010), with estimates after 2008 based on Battelle Memorial Institute (2009–2012) forecasts. The series we use is R&D that is financed and performed by industry.

The source of advertising expenditures is the U.S. Department of Commerce, Bureau of the Census (2009–2012). Prior to 2008, the estimates are advertising expenditures, and after 2008 they are advertising revenues. For years in which we have both expenditures and revenues, the patterns are the same.

The market value of U.S. business in Figure 12 is the sum of the market value of domestic corporations (FOF L213) and equity in noncorporate business (FOF B100).

To make all series comparable, intangible expenditures and market values are detrended in the same way as the series for the national accounts.

## Federal Regulatory Spending and Employment

Estimates of spending related to federal regulatory activities shown in Figure 13 are constructed by Dudley and Warren (2010), are based on the *Budget of the United States Government,* and are fiscal-year values. The main categories of regulation included in their estimates are consumer safety and health, homeland security, transportation, workplace, environment, energy, finance and banking, industry-specific regulation, and general business regulation. Agencies that primarily perform taxation, entitlement, procurement, subsidy, and credit functions are excluded from the estimates. These agencies include, for example, the Internal Revenue Service, the Social Security Administration, the Commodity Credit Corporation, and the Federal Housing Administration. Dudley and Warren (2010) also report estimates of the full-time equivalent employment required for regulatory activities, which is shown in Figure 14.

## References

Arellano, Cristina, Yan Bai, and Patrick Kehoe, 2011, "Financial Markets and Fluctuations in Uncertainty," Federal Reserve Bank of Minneapolis, mimeo.

Barro, Robert J., and Charles J. Redlick, 2011, "Macroeconomic Effects from Government Purchases and Taxes," *Quarterly Journal of Economics,* 126(1): 51–102.

Battelle Memorial Institute, 2009–2012, "The Source-Performer Matrix: Estimated Distribution of U.S. R&D Funds," *Global R&D Funding Forecast* (www.battelle.org).

Berger, David, 2012, "Countercyclical Restructuring and Jobless Recoveries," Yale University, mimeo.

Bloom, Nicholas, 2009, "The Impact of Uncertainty Shocks," *Econometrica,* 77(3): 623–685.

Bloom, Nicholas, Max Floetotto, Nir Jaimovich, Itay Saporta-Eksten, and Stephen Terry, 2011, "Really Uncertain Business Cycles," Stanford University, mimeo.

Board of Governors of the Federal Reserve System, 1945–2005, *Flow of Funds Accounts of the United States,* Statistical Release Z.1 (Washington, DC: Federal Reserve System).

Braun, R. Anton, 1994, "Tax Disturbances and Real Economic Activity in the Postwar United States," *Journal of Monetary Economics,* 33(3): 441–462.

Campello, Murillo, John R. Graham, and Campbell R. Harvey, 2010, "The Real Effects of Financial Constraints: Evidence from a Financial Crisis," *Journal of Financial Economics,* 97(3): 470–487.

Chari, V. V., Patrick J. Kehoe, and Ellen R. McGrattan, 2007, "Business Cycle Accounting," *Econometrica,* 75(3): 781–836.

Chernousov, Michael, Susan E. Fleck, and John Glaser, 2009, "Productivity Trends in Business Cycles: A Visual Essay," *Monthly Labor Review,* 132(6): 50–63.

Corrado, Carol A., Charles R. Hulten, and Daniel E. Sichel, 2005, "Measuring Capital and Technology: An Expanded Framework," in Carol Corrado,

John Haltiwanger, and Daniel Sichel (eds.), *Measuring Capital in the New Economy* (Chicago: University of Chicago Press).

Corrado, Carol A., Charles R. Hulten, and Daniel E. Sichel, 2006, "Intangible Capital and Economic Growth," Finance and Economics Discussion Series, 2006–24, Divisions of Research and Statistics and Monetary Affairs, Federal Reserve Board, Washington, DC.

Crain, Nicole V., and W. Mark Crain, 2010, "The Impact of Regulatory Costs on Small Firms," U.S. Small Business Administration, Office of Advocacy (www.sba.gov).

Dudley, Susan, and Melinda Warren, 2010, "A Decade of Growth in the Regulators' Budget: An Analysis of the U.S. Budget for Fiscal Years 2010 and 2011," *2011 Annual Report, Regulators' Budget Report 32,* Weidenbaum Center on the Economy, Government and Public Policy, Washington University and Regulatory Studies Center, George Washington University, Washington, DC.

*Economist,* 2012, "Over-regulated America," February 18–24.

Galí, Jordi, and Thijs van Rens, 2010, "The Vanishing Procyclicality of Labor Productivity," CREI, Universitat Pompeu Fabra, mimeo.

Garin, Julio, Michael Pries, and Eric Sims, 2011, "Reallocation and the Changing Nature of Economic Fluctuations," University of Notre Dame, mimeo.

Gertler, Mark, and Nobuhiro Kiyotaki, 2010, "Financial Intermediation and Credit Policy in Business Cycle Analysis," in Benjamin M. Friedman and Michael Woodford (eds.), *Handbook of Monetary Economics,* Vol. 3, pp. 547–599 (Amsterdam: Elsevier).

Hansen, Gary D., 1985, "Indivisible Labor and the Business Cycle," *Journal of Monetary Economics,* 16(3): 309–327.

Hodrick, Robert J., and Edward C. Prescott, 1997, "Postwar U.S. Business Cycles: An Empirical Investigation," *Journal of Money, Credit and Banking,* 29(1): 1–16.

Holman, Corey, Bobbie Joyeux, and Christopher Kask, 2008, "Labor Productivity Trends Since 2000, by Sector and Industry," *Monthly Labor Review,* 131(2): 64–82.

Hulten, Charles, 2010, "Decoding Microsoft: Intangible Capital as a Source of Company Growth," NBER Working Paper 15799.

Kydland, Finn, and Edward C. Prescott, 1982, "Time to Build and Aggregate Fluctuations," *Econometrica*, 50(6): 1345–1370.

Mathews, Anna Wilde, 2011, "Walked into a Lamppost? Hurt While Crocheting? Help Is on the Way," *Wall Street Journal*, September 13.

McGrattan, Ellen R., 1994, "The Macroeconomic Effects of Distortionary Taxation," *Journal of Monetary Economics*, 33(3): 573–601.

McGrattan, Ellen R., forthcoming, "Capital Taxation During the U.S. Great Depression," *Quarterly Journal of Economics*.

McGrattan, Ellen R., and Edward C. Prescott, 2010, "Unmeasured Investment and the Puzzling U.S. Boom in the 1990s," *American Economic Journal: Macroeconomics*, 2(4): 88–123.

Mulligan, Casey, 2011, "Rising Labor Productivity During the 2008–9 Recession," NBER Working Paper 17584.

National Science Foundation, 2010, Division of Science Resources Statistics, *National Patterns of R&D Resources: 2008 Data Update* (www.nsf.gov/statistics/nsf10314).

Ohanian, Lee E., 2010, "The Economic Crisis from a Neoclassical Perspective," *Journal of Economic Perspectives*, 24(4): 45–66.

Ohanian, Lee E., and Andrea Raffo, 2012, "Aggregate Hours Worked in OECD Countries: New Measurement and Implications for Business Cycles," *Journal of Monetary Economics*, 59(1): 40–56.

Prescott, Edward C., Alexander Ueberfeldt, and Simona Cociuba, 2005, "U.S. Hours and Productivity Behavior Using CPS Hours Worked Data: 1959-I to 2005-II," Manuscript, Research Department, Federal Reserve Bank of Minneapolis.

Schaal, Edouard, 2012, "Uncertainty, Productivity and Unemployment in the Great Recession," Federal Reserve Bank of Minneapolis, mimeo.

Taylor, John B., 2011, "Macroeconomic Lessons from the Great Deviation," in Daron Acemoglu and Michael Woodford (eds.), *NBER Macroeconomics Annual 2010*, Vol. 25, pp. 387–395 (Chicago: University of Chicago Press).

U.S. Department of Commerce, Bureau of the Census, 2009–2012. *Statistical Abstract of the United States* (Washington, DC: U.S. Government Printing Office).

U.S. Department of Commerce, Bureau of Economic Analysis, 1929–2011, National Income and Product Accounts, *Survey of Current Business* (Washington, DC: U.S. Government Printing Office).

CHAPTER 7

# Why the U.S. Economy Has Failed to Recover and What Policies Will Promote Growth

KYLE F. HERKENHOFF AND LEE E. OHANIAN

## 1. Introduction

This study examines the recovery from the 2008–2009 recession from the perspective of the neoclassical growth model, thus extending Ohanian's (2010) neoclassical analysis of the downturn phase of this recession. This paper documents the characteristics and features of the recovery, identifies the sources of economic weakness, discusses the possible impact of economic policies on the recovery, and provides an assessment of what types of policies may help accelerate the speed of the recovery and restore prosperity.

Our main finding is that the recovery from the recession has been very weak compared to recoveries from other postwar recessions, particularly in the restoration of jobs. The failure of jobs to recover is indeed puzzling from the perspective of standard economics, as worker productivity is very high and the health of the banking sector has improved considerably since 2008–09. One has to go back to the Great Depression to find such a comparatively weak recovery in the labor market, when jobs also were very slow to recover despite high worker productivity and the restoration of the banking system.

Lucas and Rapping (1972), Alchian (1970), and Cole and Ohanian (2004), among others, argued that government policies that cartelized product and labor markets and resulted in abnormally high real wages and relative prices in many sectors of the 1930s U.S. economy were to blame for the failure of jobs to return after 1933. However, the economic policies that depressed job creation in the 1930s are not the same as those today. In contrast, there have been a number of labor-related, tax-related, and spending-related policy mistakes that in our view have contributed to the slow recovery. Labor-related policies such as poorly designed unemployment benefits, visa requirements for entrepreneurs who hire Americans, and visa requirements for skilled workers are impeding job growth. The ever-changing landscape of taxes and uncertainty over future unfunded liabilities are also generating disincentives for companies to invest in capital and long-term employment relationships.

We discuss several reforms, including redesigning unemployment benefits to better reward job finding rather than rewarding non-employment, reforming residency requirements for immigrants, committing to a simpler bipartisan tax scheme to widen the tax base and eliminate uncertainty, encouraging the use of private retirement accounts for a portion of Social Security, and allowing current Medicare recipients to choose between private insurance and Medicare. All of these policies would limit further government spending and obligations while generating the jobs and investment necessary for long-run growth.

## 2. The Failure of Economic Recovery

In this section we measure per capita real output, consumption, investment, government spending, and labor input relative to their respective trends to identify how these variables changed over the recession phase, and how much recovery has occurred since June 2009, which is the trough of the 2008–09 recession as identified by the National Bureau of Economic Research's (NBER) business cycle dating committee. We begin with hours worked, which includes changes in both employment and hours per worker, and thus is the best measure of labor input. This is presented in Figure 1. Note that hours worked declines considerably during the recession, but

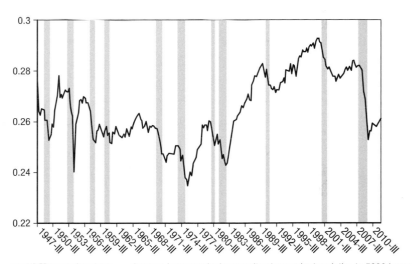

NBER recession dates —— Average hours worked per capita at annual rate relative to 5200 hours

**Figure 1.** Hours worked per capita relative to 5200 hours, annualized and seasonally adjusted.

*Source:* Update of Prescott, Ueberfeldt, Cociuba (2005).

then continues to decline several months after the NBER trough, finally falling to a nearly three-decade low. The magnitude of this decline during the 2009 recession is more severe than of any other U.S. postwar recession, except perhaps the 1953 recession, which reflected in part the end of the Korean War expansion. The recovery in hours worked following the 2008–09 recession is extraordinarily slow, which we discuss in detail below (see the discussion below for Table 2).

Output, consumption, and investment also declined more in 2008–09 than in past recessions, and these data are plotted in Figure 2.[1] As in the case of hours worked, investment also has not recovered back to its pre-recession trend. To see this more clearly, Table 1 presents deviations from trend in these macroeconomic variables for all postwar recessions. Investment and hours have the largest declines relative to other recessions. The decline in output and consumption were roughly in line with their respective postwar averages, but the drop in hours was disproportionately larger. The fact that hours fell considerably more than output suggests that the workers who were displaced during the recession were primarily low-skilled/low-productivity workers.

Table 2 (see page 161) compares the variables during the first two years of recovery following the June 2009 trough.[2] The current recession stands out in sharp contrast from others, not only in terms of the magnitude of the decline during the recession, but

---

1. These national accounts are calculated using similar formulas to Chari, Kehoe, and McGrattan (2006), which involves reclassifying several accounts, adjusting for sales taxes, detrending by a growth rate of 2 percent per annum, and expressing each account as a per capita number.

2. The 1957 and 1980 recessions are omitted due to the proximity of the next recession.

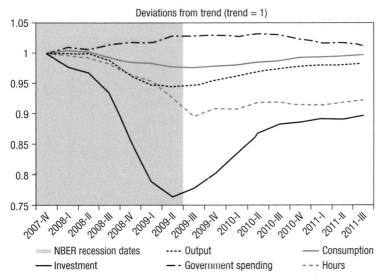

**Figure 2.** Business cycle accounts, per capita and detrended, deviations from trend.

*Source:* Bureau of Economic Analysis (BEA), Bureau of Labor Statistics (BLS), and authors' calculations.

also in the *persistence* of the decline during recovery, particularly in hours. Hours remain eight percent below trend two years after the recession trough. We will discuss some hypotheses concerning this abnormally large deviation from trend below. Investment is also well below trend compared to other recoveries, except perhaps the recession of the mid-1970s, when energy prices rose considerably.

These tables and figures present a systematic pattern of economic weakness reflecting a severe recession and relatively little recovery from that recession, particularly in terms of labor input. We analyze the failure of the labor market to recover in more detail by presenting data on employment, which is the measure of labor input that is most commonly cited in media reports of jobs, and

**Table 1.** Percent deviation, peak to trough.

| | *Percent deviation from trend at trough (%)* | | | | |
| | *Output* | *Consumption* | *Investment* | *Government Spending* | *Hours* |
| --- | --- | --- | --- | --- | --- |
| 1949-IV | −4.24 | −1.47 | −11.95 | −2.40 | −4.17 |
| 1954-II | −5.19 | −1.20 | −10.21 | −11.03 | −4.04 |
| 1958-II | −7.82 | −4.95 | −12.94 | 0.73 | −4.55 |
| 1961-I | −3.00 | −1.25 | −6.19 | −0.95 | −0.39 |
| 1970-IV | −4.01 | −0.74 | −8.78 | −5.60 | −3.89 |
| 1975-I | −7.61 | −3.13 | −22.10 | −1.08 | −4.80 |
| 1980-III | −3.95 | −1.82 | −14.50 | −1.06 | −2.72 |
| 1982-IV | −6.39 | −0.48 | −17.29 | −0.24 | −3.95 |
| 1991-I | −2.70 | −1.72 | −8.64 | 0.42 | −2.14 |
| 2001-IV | −1.73 | −1.07 | −4.26 | 0.83 | −2.42 |
| **2009-II** | **−5.48** | **−2.21** | **−23.55** | **2.84** | **−7.45** |

| | *Average postwar percent deviation from trend at trough (%)* | | | | |
| | *Output* | *Consumption* | *Investment* | *Government Spending* | *Hours* |
| --- | --- | --- | --- | --- | --- |
| **Average** | −4.66 | −1.78 | −11.69 | −2.04 | −3.31 |

*Source:* BEA, BLS, and authors' calculations.

which is available for a longer time period.[3] Figure 3 shows the employment-population ratio between 1947 and 2011. The figure shows that jobs fell substantially during the 2008–09 recession, and have not come back. Likewise, Figure 4 shows the percentage change in total nonfarm employment thirty-six months after the previous business cycle peak for each post–World War II recession. The figure shows that employment for most recessions recovers quickly, rising about 3 percent above the previous cyclical peak.

---

3. See Ohanian and Raffo (2011) for more on the measurement of labor input.

**Table 2.** Percent Deviation, Recovery.

| | *Percent deviation from trend 2 years after trough (%)* | | | | |
|---|---|---|---|---|---|
| | *Output* | *Consumption* | *Investment* | *Government Spending* | *Hours* |
| 1951-IV | 8.15 | 1.93 | 15.05 | 32.78 | 1.89 |
| 1956-II | −0.89 | 3.09 | −3.64 | −15.88 | −0.74 |
| 1963-I | 1.79 | 0.20 | 5.76 | 3.76 | −1.17 |
| 1972-IV | −1.47 | −0.03 | 3.52 | −13.45 | −3.89 |
| 1977-I | −6.17 | −2.14 | −10.48 | −6.50 | −2.00 |
| 1984-IV | 0.20 | 1.65 | 11.54 | −1.47 | 3.16 |
| 1993-I | −2.45 | −1.71 | −2.99 | −5.06 | −2.14 |
| 2003-IV | −2.99 | −3.66 | 0.14 | −0.72 | −4.15 |
| 2011-II | −1.97 | −0.49 | −10.91 | 1.63 | −8.16 |

| | *Average postwar percent deviation from trend 2 years after trough (%)* | | | | |
|---|---|---|---|---|---|
| | *Output* | *Consumption* | *Investment* | *Government Spending* | *Hours* |
| Average | −0.48 | −0.08 | 2.36 | −0.82 | −1.13 |

*Source:* BEA, BLS, and authors' calculations.

In sharp contrast, employment was 6 percent lower at the thirty-six-month stage following our most recent recession. Note that the only other recession in which there were fewer jobs at this stage was the 2000–2001 recession, which was a much milder recession, and in which there was about 1 percent fewer jobs.

A similar pattern of recovery failure also emerges by comparing employment *growth* after NBER recession troughs, which is presented in Figure 5. This figure shows that nonfarm employment grows significantly within the first two years of recovery following U.S. recessions, as in most recoveries employment grows 5 percent or more. In contrast, employment growth is well below 1 percent twenty-four months after the NBER June 2009 trough. This is the

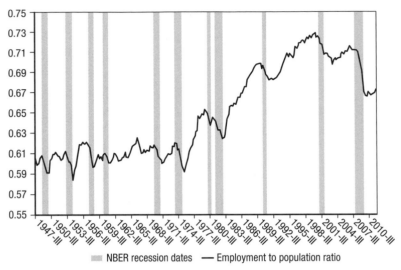

**Figure 3.** Employment over population.

*Source:* BLS, and authors' calculations.

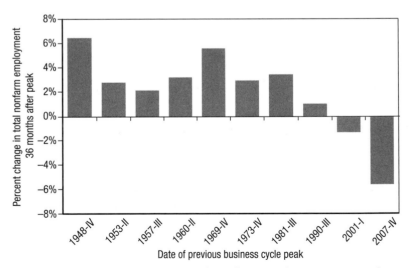

**Figure 4.** Percentage change in total nonfarm employment 36 months after the previous business cycle peak.

*Source:* BLS, and authors' calculations.

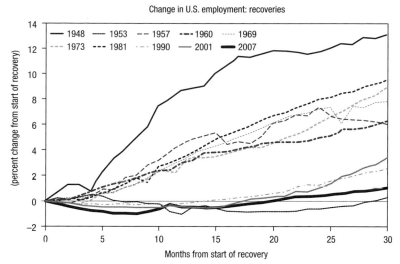

**Figure 5.** Employment over population, deviations from trend, starting at NBER recession troughs.

*Source:* BLS, and authors' calculations.

only severe postwar recession that did not exhibit strong job recovery other than the 1973–74 recession, in which very high oil prices continued following that recession.

## 3. The Failure to Recover and Labor Market Dysfunction

This section uses recent developments in diagnostic techniques for understanding why the recovery has been so weak, particularly in the labor market. This approach was recently used in Ohanian (2010), who studied the reasons why the recession phase of our economy was so severe. The approach makes use of the standard neoclassical growth model, which specifies production of final goods and services from a production function using capital and labor. The standard neoclassical growth model captures the trade-off that households face in terms of supplying labor to the market or using their time for non-market activities, and the tradeoff that households face in terms of allocating income between consumption and savings.

Diagnosing the sources of weakness in the recovery is based on the extent that the predicted relationships in the model that govern the values of consumption, investment, output, and employment differ from the actual values. This gives rise to three relationships that can be measured and compared to data. One measures the deviation between actual total factor productivity and its trend value. Another, which is called the capital market deviation, measures the deviation between the actual average return to investment in the economy and the return implied by the theory. The third is the labor market deviation, which measures the deviation between the actual return to working and the return implied by the theory. These diagnostics represent an accounting framework in that if there are no deviations when comparing the predicted values and the actual values, then the economy is growing at its trend rate. Thus, if the economy is below trend, it will manifest itself in at least one of these conditions.[4]

Using the data illustrated in Figure 1 and Table 1 we construct the deviations in these three model relationships. Figure 6 (see page 165) shows the actual values of these deviations. Values that are equal to one mean there is no deviation, whereas values below one indicate that there is a negative deviation. The figure shows

---

4. There is one other deviation, which measures changes in the allocation of income between consumption, investment, government spending, and net exports, though this deviation is typically unimportant.

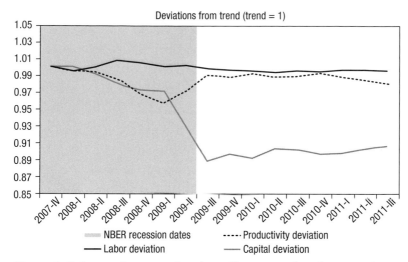

**Figure 6.** Labor wedge, capital wedge, efficiency wedge, deviation from trend.

*Source:* BEA, BLS, and authors' calculations.

that the recession of 2008–09 reflects factors that were depressing the labor market, as the labor market deviation is negative, and to a lesser extent, reflects low productivity.[5] However, the continuation of economic weakness following the June 2009 trough entirely reflects factors that are depressing the U.S. labor market, as total factor productivity has recovered. Labor productivity, which is plotted in Figure 7, has also recovered, and in fact largely has been above trend since the June 2009 trough.

Table 3 illustrates the peak to trough changes in these three diagnostic deviations for the other U.S. postwar downturns. The labor deviation is clearly disproportionately large in this recession

---

5. See also Mulligan (2009) for discussions about the initial downturn in the labor wedge.

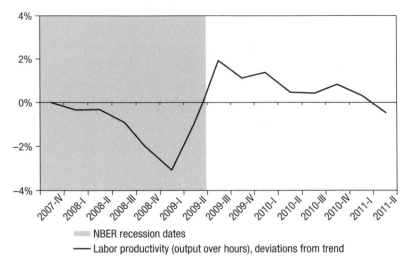

**Figure 7.** Labor productivity.
*Source:* BEA, BLS, and authors' calculations.

compared to the other U.S. downturns, and, as documented in Figure 8, the failure of this deviation to recover following a recession is unprecedented.

The large labor market distortion that is impacting the economy now is resulting in abnormally low job creation rates. The job creation rate and job destruction rate are plotted in Figure 9. The data are from the Business Dynamics Statistics (BDS) database from the Bureau of the Census. When the job creation rate falls below the job destruction rate, there is an *employment contraction.* From the figure it is clear that job creation is almost 4 percent lower than job destruction during the current recession, and has not recovered much following the recession. This is the largest shortfall in net job creation in the U.S. economy over the period 1976 to 2009 for which we have data.

**Table 3.** Wedges from Peak to Trough.

| | *Percent deviation from trend at trough (%)* | | |
|---|---|---|---|
| | *Productivity Deviation* | *Labor Deviation* | *Capital Deviation* |
| 1949-IV | −1.47 | −2.84 | −0.01 |
| 1954-II | −2.88 | −1.50 | −0.56 |
| 1958-II | −4.87 | −3.15 | −1.06 |
| 1961-I | −2.66 | 1.27 | 0.13 |
| 1970-IV | −1.22 | −1.93 | 0.04 |
| 1975-I | −4.18 | −1.76 | −1.21 |
| 1980-III | −1.99 | −1.50 | −0.92 |
| 1982-IV | −3.38 | 0.76 | −1.98 |
| 1991-I | −1.16 | −1.98 | 0.22 |
| 2001-IV | −0.03 | −2.72 | −0.45 |
| **2009-II** | **−2.89** | **−6.97** | **0.08** |
| | *Average postwar percent deviation from trend at trough (%)* | | |
| | *Productivity Deviation* | *Labor Deviation* | *Capital Deviation* |
| **Average** | −2.38 | −1.53 | −0.58 |

*Source:* BEA, BLS, and authors' calculations.

These diagnostics indicate that our lackluster recovery is almost entirely due to a distorted labor market in which too few jobs are being created. This significant job creation distortion is pathological, as on the labor supply side, the incentive to work should be high, reflecting the fact that worker productivity is very high and consumption is well below trend. Low job creation is also a puzzle on the labor demand side, as firm profitability has recovered considerably following the recession, which suggests that hiring should also expand. The rebound in profitability is shown in Figure 10, which plots non-financial and financial corporate profits between 1951 and 2011.

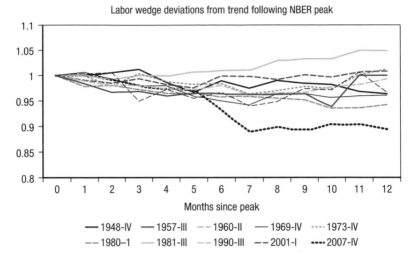

**Figure 8.** Postwar labor wedges, deviation from trend following NBER peak.

*Source:* BEA, BLS, and authors' calculations.

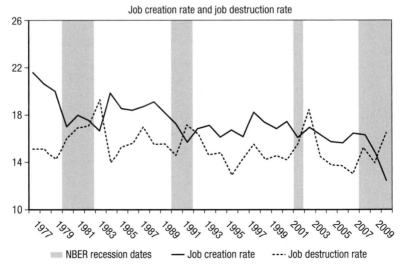

**Figure 9.** Job creation rate and job destruction rate.

*Source:* Business Dynamics Statistics (BDS).

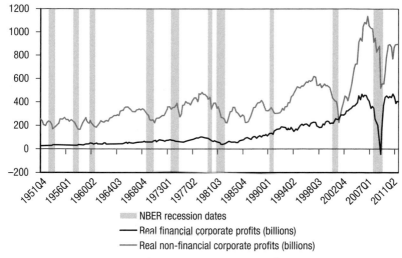

**Figure 10.**   Corporate profits, deflated by GDP deflator.

*Source:* National Income and Product Accounts (NIPA), flow of funds, and authors' calculations.

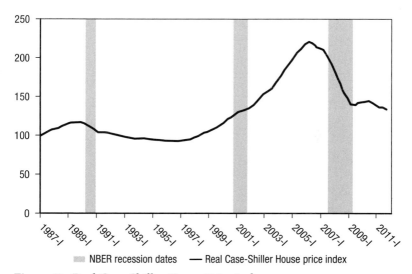

**Figure 11.**   Real Case-Shiller House Price Index.

*Source:* BEA, St. Louis Federal Reserve economic data, and authors' calculations.

The role of the housing bust, as shown by the Case-Shiller Price Index in Figure 11, and the reduced demand for construction workers may be key for understanding the persistence of unemployment in the 2007-IV recession. Boldrin, et al. (2012, in progress) uses input output relationships to measure the impact of the initial housing bust on employment and output in other sectors. In his model simulations, the construction sector shock is able to explain 51.9 percent of the drop in total employment, peak to trough. These results suggest the possibility that the economy is not reallocating labor from the construction and related industries to expanding industries.

To obtain a better understanding about the failure of our job market to recover, and the extent that labor is being reallocated from declining sectors to expanding sectors, Figure 12 shows the change in employment since the 2007:IV peak prior to the 2008–09 recession for construction, manufacturing, trade, finance, education and health, and government, while Figure 13 shows the change in employment since the June 2009 trough for these sectors. The construction sector is by far the most depressed sector, followed by the financial sector and government sector. While not depicted, the decline in government employment is mainly due to cutbacks at the state and local levels. The expanding sectors are in education and health services. However, their gains are not as robust as in past recessions, which is surprising considering the changing demographics in the United States. Figure 13 shows that manufacturing and trade have added little employment since the trough, but as is clear from other postwar recessions, manufacturing has never been the leader in creating jobs. Figure 13 also sheds additional light on the inefficiency associated with attempts to stimulate manufacturing. Specifically, the cost of creating a manufacturing job is $61,339, and, to put this in perspective, the cost of

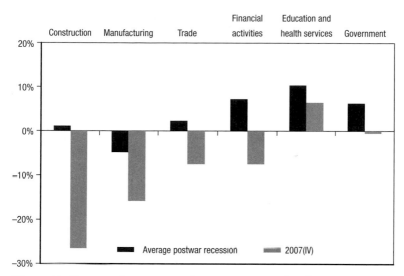

**Figure 12.** Percent change in employment 36 months after peak.
*Source:* BLS, and authors' calculations.

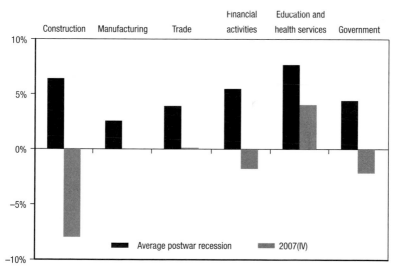

**Figure 13.** Percent change in employment 24 months after trough.
Source: BLS, and authors' calculations.

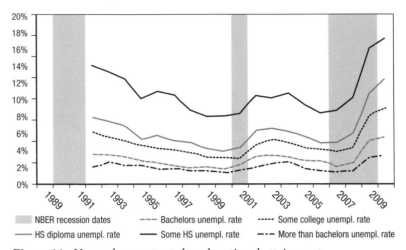

**Figure 14.** Unemployment rate by educational attainment.
*Source:* Current Population Survey (CPS), and authors' calculations.

creating a banking job is $51,444.[6] Thus, the failure of job creation reflects continuing weakness in one or two key sectors, combined with the inability of the unemployed to productively match in new sectors.

The apparent inability to move workers from depressed sectors, such as construction, to expanding sectors, such as health care and energy, leads us to explore the skill characteristics of the unemployed to determine how this may be impacting labor reallocation.[7] Figure 14 shows that the unemployment rate among low-skilled (uneducated) workers is significantly higher than the unemployment rate among more-skilled (educated) workers. Despite the job flexibility associated with workers with low human capital, they also have the same twenty-six-week median duration

---

6. In 2011 dollars, average starting salary. Source: Payscale Research.
7. For regional mobility, see Herkenhoff and Ohanian (2011).

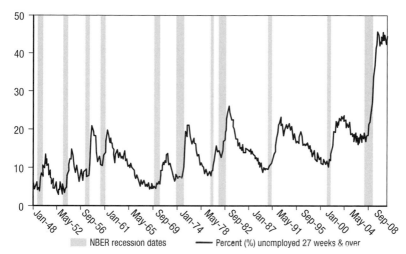

**Figure 15.** Fraction of unemployed persons without work for 27 weeks or more.

*Source:* CPS.

of unemployment as those with bachelor's degrees. Figure 15 illustrates the fraction of long-term unemployed persons—those who have been unemployed for longer than twenty-seven weeks. This number is the highest it has ever been in any postwar recession by a factor of two. The most obvious reason for this is that unemployment benefits last for ninety-nine weeks, the longest length of benefits in the postwar period. While not discussed in detail here, research in the 1990s showed that unemployment benefits can have a significant impact on unemployment durations.[8]

Figure 16 provides further evidence on the skill level of the unemployed by plotting the median wage of unemployed workers. This figure shows that the immediate previous wage rate of the unem-

---

8. See Ljungqvist and Sargent (1998) for more on unemployment durations and unemployment benefits.

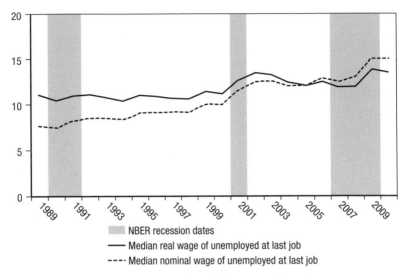

**Figure 16.** Average wage rate at last job for unemployed persons.
*Source:* CPS, and authors' calculations.

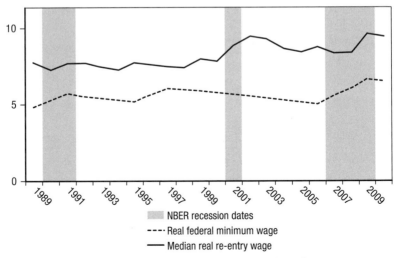

**Figure 17.** Average wage rate at last job for unemployed persons.
*Source:* Congressional Records, CPS, and authors' calculations.

ployed is quite low, at about $12 per hour. And as documented by Jacobson, Lelonde, and Sullivan (1993) and Davis and von Wachter (2011), workers who become unemployed during major recessions suffer immediate and large declines in the value of their human capital. They find that the average workers' income declines by up to 30 percent following a layoff. We follow their empirical findings to calculate a re-entry wage equal to 30 percent less than the median wage of unemployed workers, which is the wage that a typical unemployed person can expect to earn upon finding a new job. Figure 17 plots the real median re-entry wage against the real federal minimum wage, which was hiked in 2007 to $5.85 from $5.15 and hiked again in 2008 to $6.55 and raised once more in 2009 to $7.25. The picture shows that the re-entry wage and federal minimum wage are within $3 of each other.[9] Since human capital continues to deteriorate for the long-term unemployed, many of the roughly six million long-term unemployed who are around or below the median re-entry wage may be priced out of the labor market through the minimum wage laws. As mentioned above, the ninety-nine-week unemployment benefit extension may also be playing a role in prolonging unemployment durations *and* causing human capital depreciation.[10] Taken together, these data present a clear picture of the dysfunction characterizing the labor market in which the workers being most negatively impacted by poor economic growth are those with low skill levels and low wages.

---

9. Notice that these two wages have been close to each other during each of the two prior jobless recoveries in 1992 and 2002, respectively.

10. See Ljungqvist and Sargent (1998) for more on human capital depreciation and unemployment benefits.

## 4. Economic Policies to Restore Prosperity

There are several policy reforms that would significantly benefit the U.S. economy. One is enacting broad-based tax reform and instituting fiscally responsible spending policies. The various stop-gap and temporary tax and spending measures, including the American Recovery and Reinvestment Act, cash for clunkers, home-buyers tax credit, the unpredictable and temporary extensions of the Bush tax cuts including reduced Alternative Minimum Taxes, capital gains taxes, dividend taxes, and income taxes, the expiration of the estate tax cuts, the temporary business incentives including bonus depreciation and loss-carrybacks, and the constant bargaining over the temporary payroll tax cuts and extended unemployment benefits have created uncertainty about future tax policy by driving up the federal debt and by explicitly targeting tax measures as temporary changes that would expire when the economy improved.

One consequence of these policies is that it has become very difficult for businesses to forecast future policy, and this uncertainty impacts business investment and hiring decisions. To see this, note that much of the tangible and intangible capital investments are irreversible. Human capital investments such as training new employees, come at a significant upfront cost that is paid in expectation of back-loaded benefits. According to the Employee Tenure Summary released by the BLS, the average job tenure is 4.4 years. The easy way to rationalize this tenure is that the employer spreads the initial fixed costs of hiring over as many years as possible. However, with current levels of uncertainty over the cost of long-term employment via health care costs and social security contributions, employers face the risk of incurring significant additional

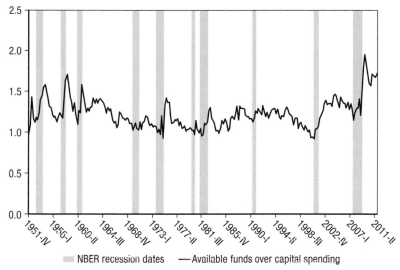

NBER recession dates — Available funds over capital spending

**Figure 18.** Cash on hand over gross investment ratio.
*Source:* BEA and flow of funds.

fixed costs. This is impacting hiring, as businesses hire fewer new employees and hire only those skilled enough to generate the necessary income that can justify the anticipated and realized fixed costs of hiring. This is one factor that is depressing employment among low-skilled workers, as the long-term low-skilled unemployment pool is presently at a record level.

Economic uncertainty also is impacting corporate investment and asset management. Figure 18 shows the cash-at-hand of U.S. corporations, which includes retained earnings, capital consumption, and dividends as a ratio of Gross Private Domestic Investment. When this ratio is above 1, corporations have more than enough cash to fund current investment. Some have hypothesized that this buffer is a necessity during a credit crunch since companies have difficulty externally financing projects, but Figure 19

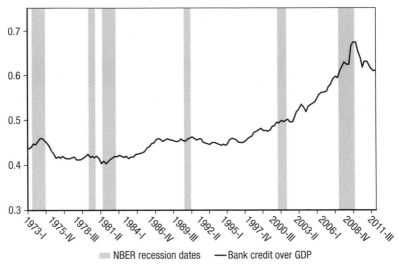

**Figure 19.** Bank credit to GDP.

*Source:* BEA and flow of funds.

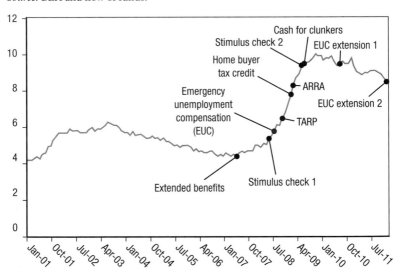

**Figure 20.** Unemployment rate with short run initiative dates.

*Source:* BLS and various news sources.

shows that bank credit to GDP has fallen only modestly since the financial crisis. An alternative reason for this cash buffer is corporate tax liabilities which are often enacted retroactively. According to congressional records, there are more than forty *live* bills that were introduced to either the senate or house in 2011 that have the potential to drastically change corporate tax laws, many of which involve substantially larger tax liabilities.

Our view is that the targeted, short-run policies that have been adopted since the Fall of 2008, and that have contributed to increasing economic uncertainty, have had little positive effect on the economy. Figure 20 shows the unemployment rate with the specific dates that various short-run policies were adopted. The graph shows no tendency for unemployment to fall around or after the times that these policies were adopted.

Better policy making requires policy that is consistent with superior long-run economic performance, rather than the short-run band-aids that have dominated policy making recently. To that end, we recommend tax reform that broadens the federal income tax base and that lowers federal income tax rates; that equalizes the tax treatment of all types of capital, including sharply reducing the corporate profits tax, which is one of the highest among advanced countries; and that shifts taxes from income to consumption. A long-term reduction in income taxes provides more stable incentives for entrepreneurs to start businesses that in turn generate more jobs and more taxable income. On the same note, a long-term reduction in corporate taxes not only provides more incentives for individuals to incorporate, which expands the tax base, it also provides incentives for existing multinational companies to invest more in the U.S. economy, which is an important factor for long-term growth and jump-starting investment. Both of these reforms can be accomplished by switching to a lower flat income tax rate with a generous deduction for households and a flat business tax for corporations.[11] Several of these tax proposals have been recommended by bipartisan tax reform committees under President George W. Bush and under President Obama.

Tax reform should be accompanied by lower government spending.[12] Figure 21 shows federal purchases and transfers between 1947 and today. Note that spending today is 24.6 percent of GDP in 2011 (both numbers are seasonally adjusted at annual rates), compared to just 20 percent as recently as 2007. Our view is that broadly addressing federal spending, including entitlements and unfunded government pension liabilities, is required to keep federal spending at a roughly constant level of GDP at no more than 20 percent. There are three programs that are a major factor in growing government spending: Medicare (general health care for the elderly), Medicaid (health care for low-income households), and Social Security (retirement benefits). The Congressional Budget Office (CBO) predicts federal spending on Medicaid and Medicare will be roughly 10 percent of GDP by 2040.[13] This would be sustainable if the programs had accrued savings since inception, but the problem is that these programs are "pay-as-you-go," meaning that the government raises the money to pay for these obligations each year, and any shortfall must be made up by either borrowing or increased government revenue. Figure 22 shows current debt held by the public over GDP, which is at a level that hasn't been seen since the arms buildup of World War II. One potential way to address these large unfunded liabilities is to allow

---

11. The word "flat" is deceiving because this will actually maintain the current progressive tax structure.

12. See Taylor (2012), Cogan and Taylor (2011), and Taylor (2009).

13. See http://www.cbo.gov/ftpdocs/93xx/doc9317/05-29-NASI_Speech.pdf.

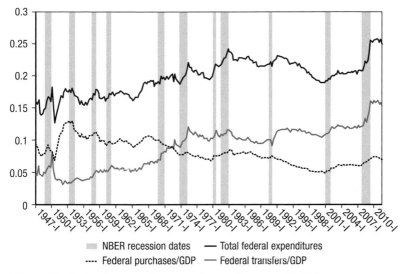

**Figure 21.** Federal expenditures and transfers over GDP.
*Source:* BEA.

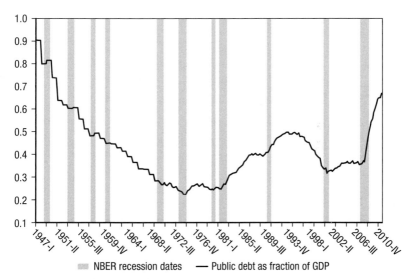

**Figure 22.** Federal debt held by public over GDP.
*Source:* BEA and Congressional Business Office (CBO).

the newly contributing generations to save part of their contributions in funded accounts that can be reinvested instead of simply redistributed. To limit the costs of Medicare, seniors should be given the choice of partially subsidized private health care insurance or the traditional Medicare coverage. With a capped subsidy, this will allow the government to curb long-run costs for those who opt for different plans that tailor to their particular needs.

Reforming unemployment insurance would benefit the labor market by improving incentives to reward job-taking and retraining. Instead of subsidizing non-employment, policy should be more explicitly focused on employment efforts and rewarding those who actually find jobs. The current ninety-nine weeks of employment benefits has changed job search incentive for the nearly 7.6 million Americans receiving the benefits. It is empirically documented that unemployment exit rate spikes as benefits expire.[14] Recently, Casey Mulligan (2011) has argued that the growing social safety net explains a large fraction of reduced employment. Replacement rates of total income for non-employed persons have roughly doubled from 13 percent to 26 percent since the onset of the recession, which means the incentives to work are lower. Most of these programs are means-tested, which favors those with lower income and acts as a tax on those who raise their income.[15] Mulligan explains as much as two-thirds of the reduction in labor supply through this channel, suggesting that for many

---

14. See Katz and Meyer (1990) for one such study.

15. Some examples include the Home Affordable Modification Program (HAMP) and the Bankruptcy Reform Law. For more on HAMP, see Herkenhoff and Ohanian (2011) and for more on the unemployment benefit aspect of mortgages, see Herkenhoff and Ohanian (2012).

non-workers the cost of re-entering the labor force, including the opportunity cost of their time, is greater than the pecuniary benefits. A step in the right direction is to reform unemployment benefits by shifting some funds into retraining such as scholarships and financial aid for post secondary education, especially for those attempting to attain science, technology, engineering, and medical (STEM) jobs that historically generate long-term growth. Job-finding bonuses, rather than typical unemployment insurance, are another way of incentivizing *job acceptance* rather than incentivizing non-employment.

Immigration reform would also benefit the economy by expanding our skilled workforce. According to the Survey of Earned Doctorates, as of 1966 roughly 20 percent of doctorate degrees were awarded to temporary residents. As of 2008, over 40 percent of doctorate degrees were awarded to temporary residents. A policy that grants residency to those with advanced degrees who live here and start businesses that employ workers domestically is a win-win for the United States. Not only does it boost job creation, but it contributes to American innovation in the STEM fields which are critical for long-term growth. Providing additional tax incentives for high-skilled immigrant entrepreneurs who hire low-skilled workers is another strategy to get the economy jump-started and avoid minimum wage constraints.

## 5. Conclusion

The major factor holding back today's economy from a full recovery is labor market dysfunction in which job creation is far too low given that labor productivity is above trend, that the credit crisis is over, and that corporate profitability is relatively high. Moreover, the individuals most impacted by this labor market dysfunction are those workers with the lowest skills and wages.

This labor market dysfunction reflects a number of labor-related, tax-related, and spending-related policy mistakes that have contributed to the slow recovery. We propose several long-term reforms, including redesigning unemployment benefits to incentivize job finding instead of non-employment and to help re-train workers, creating tax breaks and providing residency for highly educated immigrants who employ Americans, committing to a broader tax reform to widen the tax base and eliminate uncertainty, allowing for private Social Security saving accounts, and giving Medicare recipients the option of private insurance. All of these policies limit further government spending and liabilities while promoting incentives to invest and hire that America needs for long-run growth.

## References

Alchian, A. A. 1970. "Information Costs, Pricing, and Resource Unemployment." In *Microeconomic Foundations of Employment and Inflation Theory.* Edmund S. Phelps (ed) New York: Norton.

Boldrin, M., C. Garriga, A. Peralta-Alva, and J. Sanchez. 2012. "Reconstructing the Great Recession." Federal Reserve Bank of St. Louis Working Paper.

Chari, V. V., P. Kehoe, and E. R. McGrattan. 2006. "Business Cycle Accounting." Federal Reserve Bank of Minneapolis Working Paper.

Cogan, J. F., and J. B. Taylor. 2011. "What the Government Purchases Multiplier Actually Multiplied in the 2009 Stimulus Package." Manuscript.

Cole, H. L., and L. E. Ohanian. 2004. "New Deal Policies and the Persistence of the Great Depression: A General Equilibrium Analysis." *Journal of Political Economy.*

Davis, S. J., and T. von Wachter. 2011. "Recessions and the Cost of Job Loss." NBER Working Paper No. 17638.

Herkenhoff, K. F., and L. E. Ohanian. 2011. "Labor Market Dysfunction." *Cato Journal.*

Herkenhoff, K. F., and L. E. Ohanian. 2012. "Foreclosure Delay and US Unemployment." Manuscript.

Jacobson, L. S., R. J. Lelonde, and D. G. Sullivan. 1993. "Earnings Losses of Displaced." *American Economic Review.*

Katz, L., and B. D. Meyer. 1990. "The Impact of the Potential Duration of Unemployment Benefits on the Duration of Unemployment." *Journal of Public Economics.*

Ljunqvist, L., and T. Sargent. 1998. "The European Unemployment Dilemma." *Journal of Political Economy.*

Lucas, R. E., and L. A. Rapping. 1972. "Unemployment in the Great Depression: Is There a Full Explanation?" *Journal of Political Economy.*

Mulligan, C. B. 2009. "Aggregate Implications of Labor Market Distortions: The Recession of 2008–9 and Beyond." Manuscript.

Mulligan, C. B. 2011. "Means-Tested Subsidies and Economic Performance Since 2007." NBER Working Paper 17445.

Ohanian, L. E. 2010. "The Economic Crisis from a Neoclassical Perspective." *Journal of Economic Perspectives.*

Ohanian, L. E., and A. Raffo. 2011. "Hours Worked over the Business Cycle in OECD Countries, 1960–2010." Manuscript.

Prescott, E., A. Ueberfeldt, and S. Cociuba. 2005. "U.S. Hours and Productivity Behavior using CPS Hours Worked Data: 1959-I to 2005-II." Federal Reserve Bank of Minneapolis Working Paper.

Taylor, J. B. 2009. "Getting Off Track—How Government Actions and Interventions Caused, Prolonged, and Worsened the Financial Crisis." Hoover Institution, Stanford University.

Taylor, J. B. 2012. "First Principles: Five Keys to Restoring America's Prosperity." W.W. Norton & Company.

# Chapter 8

# Restoring Sound Economic Policy: Three Views*

## Alan Greenspan, George P. Shultz, and John H. Cochrane

Three panelists, Alan Greenspan, George Shultz, and John Cochrane, share their views on restoring sound economic policy and then answer questions from the audience.

### Prepared Remarks

**Alan Greenspan (AG):** I'm going to restrict myself to just two recommendations on policy, both of which, I think, have fairly large payoffs and a remote possibility of actually occurring, which is not an irrelevant consideration these days.

The first recommendation addresses probably the worst economic policy that we have devised in this country, and it's called the H1-B immigration quotas. Now, the H1-B immigration quotas,

---

* This article is the edited transcript of remarks and discussion during the course of the conference "Restoring Robust Economic Growth in America" at Hoover Institution, Stanford University, on December 2, 2011.

as I think you're all acutely aware, essentially limit the number of skilled workers entering the United States. This has a number of very interesting consequences, none of which are good.

As the infrastructure of our capital stock gets even more highly technical and productive, we need an ever-increasing supply of intellectually competent and well-trained people to staff the system. But because of the H1-B policy, we are not bringing in people to fill the gap that our education system has created. We have an inadequate supply of domestically-educated people with the skills needed to run the complex technical system we have. Moreover, we're in the discouraging position of experiencing declining trends in the education of our students.

In 1995 there was a study of this country's students' performance in math and science compared to the rest of the world. It was shocking: we turned out to be down somewhere in the middle, after excelling at everything we did previously. These students are now showing up in the labor force and their average incomes are below what they should be relative to similar cohorts of earlier periods. If you believe that incomes do relate to productivity, we are replacing the most productive part of our workforce (the baby boomers are basically retiring), with the least productive. Something has to give. So we're shutting down the number of people coming in at the highly-skilled level, and doing potentially grave damage to the productivity of the capital stock. You can see the differential in hiring. Siemens can't hire enough skilled people, while there's a huge excess supply of others. So this is where we stand on a very significant part of the economic system, which is not good.

No one ever really thinks about how the H1-B program subsidizes every one of the educated people in this room. If you look at who is being kept out, it is those people who would compete with us—people in, say, the upper 15 to 20 percent of the highly educated population. This means that the incomes of such educated people are higher than they should be. And this is one of the reasons why we have such a tremendously skewed distribution of income in this country. Effectively, we're subsidizing those with upper incomes and we shouldn't be.

What all of the studies show is that from a political perspective or from a sociological point of view, the issue is not the absolute level of income for society. It's how you fare relative to everybody else. Keeping up with the Joneses is one of the most profoundly significant propensities of human behavior that I know. And I believe that, were we to eliminate H1-B, we could dramatically alter a goodly amount of the problems that we have with respect to income distribution. I see no reason at this stage to continue it. Now I am told that it's the labor unions who insist that it be in place. But I've never heard of a reason why, because the people who the labor unions represent are not the people affected by this. I cannot understand what is in it for anybody in this country. I therefore conclude that it's the worst possible policy with which we are dealing.

The second recommendation is to start over on Dodd-Frank, the new financial regulatory law. Dodd-Frank has the very fascinating problem of being un-implementable. It requires almost two hundred so-called rulings, which imply fairly detailed analysis of particular aspects of the financial system. It requires that some generalized principles, which are stipulated in the law, be implemented by one or more regulatory agencies, often jointly, yet it doesn't specify how; it just says to do it. The problem is basically that there are five or ten specific edicts—major changes in the financial system—which are contradictory in certain cases and based upon a false concept of the way the system works. And so we're finding at this particular stage that they are not being implemented.

The reason is not difficult to explain. When I was at the Federal Reserve Board, if we did ten rulings a year, that was a full work-load. To now look at a backlog of two hundred to three hundred rulings that are required by law is an inconceivable venture, which would at least be desirable if the concepts of the way the system works were correct. But they aren't.

For example, soon after the law was passed, a billion-dollar asset-backed securities offering was to be made by the Ford Motor Credit Company. For such an offering, the new law requires that credit rating agencies have to certify—put a credit rating on—particular securities. The trouble is that the new Dodd-Frank law specified that the credit rating agencies were partially liable for their opinions. So what happened? Well, what would you expect to happen? Ford Credit couldn't find a credit rating agency. And there was a billion dollars worth of cars sitting out there, which were not going to be financed. So what did they do? Instead of trying to get the law changed, which was inconceivable, they did something very clever. I'm not sure it's legal, but the Securities and Exchange Commission (SEC) staff promised not to bring the issue up to the commission, so the commission would not have to con-front the problem. Effectively, the previous law stayed in existence, and to my knowledge, it's still there. Now there are innumerable hidden problems like this in the law and the sooner we decide to start from scratch, the better off this country will be.

**George Shultz (GS):** First of all, I agree with the two recommen-dations that Alan [Greenspan] has made so effectively. I'll only add that, with the poor quality of K–12 education in low-income-per-capita areas, we are building mal-distribution of income into the future. And once it's built in, it's going to be very hard to get it out. I think this is a crisis that we're allowing to continue. There's nothing wrong with these kids. What is wrong is the environment and the educational system in which they are trapped.

I have been heavily influenced in the economic arena by three experiences. The first experience was becoming a good friend of Milton Friedman. That was an education. Among other things, Milton taught me that people react differently to permanent income than they do to transitory income. When a change is permanent, people react, but when things are temporary, action is less likely.

The second experience was during the Nixon administration. In the Johnson period there was the Vietnam War and the Great Society, the so-called guns-and-butter society. People were justifiably worried about inflation, so there was lots of talk about wage and price guidelines as the way to avoid it. You would expect that, as a guy sitting at the University of Chicago, I would be worried about such guidelines as an intellectual and conceptual precursor to wage and price controls, and I was. I put together a conference at Chicago on guidelines and all the big hitters came. It was a fascinating conference.

So this was on my mind as I went into government service in the Nixon administration. By the early 1970s, as Director of the Office of Management and Budget, I could feel pressure coming for wage and price controls. Unbelievably, the business community was lobbying for wage controls, thinking that you could have wage controls without price controls. I decided to stake my ground and I gave a speech titled "Steady As You Go," making the argument that we had the budget under control (we did), we had a monetary policy consistent with getting inflation under control, and, with a little patience, inflation would come under control. Steady as you go. Well, I lost, spectacularly. President Nixon imposed wage and price controls, a massive intervention into the economy. It also had, I think, the predictable effect of causing the Federal Reserve to be a little easier on monetary policy than it might have been otherwise on the fallacious assumption that wage and price controls would actually do something about inflation. The result was a decade of lousy economic performance. That registered with me. Of course, I was arguing as an economist that there is a lag, so I educated myself with the phrase: an economist's lag is a politician's nightmare. You've got to feed the beast somehow during the lag.

The third experience came at the end of the 1970s and into the early eighties, when I became a friend of Ronald Reagan and wound up chairing an economic policy advisory board for him during his campaign and the first year-and-a-half of his administration. My friend, Alan, was a member of that group.

**AG:** And you were chairman.

**GS:** I was chairman. We had such stalwart members as Milton Friedman, Walter Wriston, Bill Simon, and Arthur Burns. It was a hard-hitting group of good people who knew something. We weren't telling Reagan anything he didn't know, but we helped him codify and program his ideas. The result was that when he came into office, he put into place a program compatible with prosperity without inflation. There was still the residue of price controls, so one of the first things he did within a day or two of taking office was end the controls on oil and gas. Some people warned that prices would go up. What happened? The market kicked in and prices went down.

We had inflation running in the teens and the prime interest rate was in the twenties. The economy was going nowhere. The Soviet Union was running wild in Afghanistan and elsewhere. But we put into place a program compatible with prosperity without inflation. President Reagan knowingly took a beating because he held a political umbrella over Paul Volcker to do what he needed to do at the Federal Reserve (and Paul did it magnificently). People told Reagan it would cause unemployment. They said: You're going to take a beating in the mid-term elections. As it turned out, that is exactly what happened. But he also took the view: If not us, who? If not now, when? You can't have a decent economy with inflation like this. So he was able, in effect, not to have the economist's lag become a politician's nightmare. He stood up to it and took a long view.

Those are my three experiences and, out of them, the economic policies that I think should be adopted. It's so blindingly obvious what it will take to get our economy going well again that I won't bother you by mentioning it.

Thank you.

**John Cochrane (JC):** It's a pleasure and honor to be here, especially next to such distinguished panelists.

John Taylor suggested I do something simple and easy for the panel, like cover all the troubles in Europe and the United States and how to fix them. In ten minutes. So let's go on a quick tour of Europe first.

In case you're not reading the papers, we're in financial crisis 3.0, a run on European banks stemming from their sovereign debt losses.

This is not high finance. European banks have been failing on sovereign debt since Edward III stiffed the Peruzzi in 1353. This is not a "multiple equilibrium," a run of self-confirming expectations. People are simply getting out of the way of sovereign default, since it's pretty clear that governments are at the end of the bailout rope.

By dutiful application of bad ideas and wishful thinking, the Europeans have turned a simple sovereign restructuring into a currency crisis, a fiscal crisis, a banking crisis, and now a political crisis. They could have had a lovely currency union without fiscal union. The meter in Paris measures length. The euro in Frankfurt measures value. And sovereigns default, just like companies. They could do what George Shultz beautifully called the "simple, obvious" things, and return to the kind of strong growth that would let them pay off large debts. Alas, the European Central Bank (ECB) is full in, both buying debt and lending to banks who buy debt, so now a sharp euro inflation—which is just a more damaging and wider sovereign default—seems like the most likely outcome.

How did we get here? Financial crises are runs. No run, no "crisis." Without a run, people just lose money as in the tech bust. (Let me quickly plug here Darrell Duffie's "Failure Mechanics of Dealer Banks."[1] This wonderful article explains exactly how our financial crisis was a run in dealer banks.)

For nearly one hundred years we have tried to stop runs with government guarantees—deposit insurance, generous lender of last resort, and bailouts. That patch leads to huge moral hazard. Giving a banker a bailout guarantee is like giving a teenager keys to the car and a case of whiskey. So, we appoint regulators who are

---

1. Darrell Duffie, "The Failure Mechanics of Dealer Banks," *Journal of Economic Perspectives* (2010) 24:51–72.

supposed to stop the banks from taking risks, in a hopeless arms race against smart MBAs, lawyers, and lobbyists who try to get around the regulation, and though we allow—nay, we encourage and subsidize—expansion of run-prone assets.

In Dodd-Frank, the United States simply doubled down our bets on this regime. The colossal failure of Europe's regulators to deal with something so simple and transparent as looming sovereign risk gives you some hint of how well it will work. (European banks have all along been allowed to hold sovereign debt at face value, with zero capital requirement. It's perfectly safe, right?)

The guarantee—regulate—bailout regime ends eventually, when the needed bailouts exceed governments' fiscal resources. That's where Europe is now.

And the United States is not immune. Sooner or later markets will question the tens of trillions of our government's guarantees, on top of already unsustainable deficits.

What financial system will we reconstruct from the ashes? The only possible answer seems to me to go back to the beginning. We'll have to reconstruct a financial system purged of run-prone assets, and the pretense that nobody holds risk. Don't subsidize short-term debt with a tax shield and regulatory preference; tax it; or ban it for anything close to "too big to fail." Fix the contractual flaws that make shadow bank liabilities prone to runs.

Here we are in a golden moment, because technology can circumvent all the standard objections. It is said that people need liquid assets, and banks must borrow short and lend long to provide such assets. But now, you could pay for coffee with an electronic transfer of mutual fund shares. The fund could hold stocks, or mortgage-backed securities. Nobody ever ran on a mutual fund. With instant communication, liquidity need no longer coincide with fixed value and first-come first-serve guarantees.

We also now have interest-paying reserves. The government can supply as many liquid assets as anyone wants with no inflation. We can live the Friedman rule.

Short-term debt is also the key to government crises. Greece is not in trouble because it can't borrow one year's deficits. It's in trouble because it can't roll over existing debt. Governments can be financed by coupon-only bonds with no principal repayment, thereby eliminating rollover risk and crises. The new European treaty, along with wishing governments would mend their spending ways, should at least insist on long-maturity debt.

You may say this is radical. But the guarantee—regulate—bailout regime will soon be gone. There really is no choice. The only reason to keep the old regime is to keep the subsidies and bailouts coming. Which of course is what the banks want.

On to the United States:

Why are we stagnating? I don't know. I don't think anyone knows, really. That's why we're here at this fascinating conference.

Nothing on the conventional macro policy agenda reflects a clue why we're stagnating. Score policy by whether its implicit diagnosis of the problem makes any sense.

The "jobs" bill. Even if there were a ghost of a chance of building new roads and schools in less than two years, do we have 9 percent unemployment because we stopped spending on roads and schools? No. Do we have 9 percent unemployment because we fired lots of state workers? No.

Taxing the rich is the new hot idea. But do we have 9 percent unemployment—of anything but tax lawyers and lobbyists—because the capital gains rate is too low? Besides, in this room we know that total marginal rates matter, not just average federal income taxes of Warren Buffett. Greg Mankiw figured his marginal tax rate at 93 percent including federal, state, local, and estate taxes.[2] And even he forgot about sales, excise, and corporate taxes. Is 93 percent too low, and the cause of unemployment?

The Fed is debating QE3. Or is it 5? And promising zero interest rates all the way to the third year of the Malia Obama administration. All to lower long rates ten basis points through some segmented-market magic. But do we really have 9 percent unemployment because 3 percent mortgages with 3 percent inflation are strangling the economy from lack of credit? Or because the market is screaming for three-year bonds, but Treasury issued at ten years instead? Or because $1.5 trillion of excess reserves aren't enough to mediate transactions?

I posed this question to a somewhat dovish Federal Reserve Bank president recently. He answered succinctly, "Aggregate demand is inadequate. We fill it." Really? That's at least coherent. I read the same model as an undergraduate. But as a diagnosis, it seems an awfully simplistic, uni-causal, uni-dimensional view of prosperity. Medieval doctors had four humors, not just one.

Of course in some sense we are still suffering the impact of the 2008 financial crisis. Reinhart and Rogoff are endlessly quoted that recessions following financial crises are longer.[3] But why? That observation could just mean that policy responses to financial crises are particularly wrongheaded.

In sum, the patient is having a heart attack. The doctor is debating whether to give him a double espresso or a nip of brandy. And most likely, the espresso is decaf and the brandy watered.

---

2. http://gregmankiw.blogspot.com/2008/10/blog-post.html.

3. Carmen M. Reinhart and Kenneth S. Rogoff, *This Time is Different: Eight Centuries of Financial Folly* (Princeton: Princeton University Press, 2011).

So what if this really is not a "macro" problem? What if this is Lee Ohanian's great depression—not about money, short-term interest rates, taxes, inadequately stimulating (!) deficits, but a disease of tax rates, social programs that pay people not to work, and a "war on business"? Perhaps this is the beginning of eurosclerosis. (See Bob Lucas's brilliant Milliman lecture for a chilling exposition of this view.)[4]

If so, the problem is heart disease. If so, macro tools cannot help. If so, the answer is, "Get out of the way."

People hate this answer. They want to know, "What would you do?" "What's the bold new plan?" "What's the big new idea?" "Where is the new Keynes?" They want FDR, jutting his chin out, leading us away from the fear of fear itself.

Alas, the microeconomy is a garden, not an army. It grows with property rights, rule of law, simple and non-distorting taxes, transparent rules-based regulations, a functional education system—all of George's "simple, obvious steps"—not the Big Plan for the political campaign of a Great Leader. You need to weed a garden, not just pour on the latest fertilizer. Our garden is full of weeds. (And our politics are full of fertilizer!) Yes, it was full of weeds before, but at least we know that pulling the weeds helps.

Or maybe there is something macro can do. This conference, and our fellow economists, are chock-full of brilliant new ideas both macro and micro. But how do we apply new ideas? Here I think we economists are often a bit arrogant. The step from "Wow, my last paper is cool" to "The government should spend a trillion

---

4. Robert Lucas, "The U.S. Recession of 2007–2011?" http://www.econ.washington.edu/EconomicsMillimanLecture.htm.

dollars on my idea" seems to take about fifteen minutes. Ten in Cambridge.

Compare the scientific evidence on fiscal stimulus to that on global warming. Even if you're a skeptic on global warming, it's clear that compared to global warming, our evidence for stimulus—including coherent theory and decisive empirical work—is on the level of, "Hey, it's pretty hot outside." And compared to mortgage modification plans, strange "unconventional" monetary policy, the latest creative fix-the-banks plan, and huge labor market interventions, even stimulus is well-documented.

There are new ideas and great new ideas. But there are also bad new ideas, lots of warmed-over bad old ideas, and good ideas that happen to be wrong. We don't know which is which. If we apply anything like the standards we would demand of anyone else's trillion-dollar government policy to our new ideas, the result for policy, now, must again be, stick with what works and the stuff we know is broken and get out of the way.

But keep working on those new ideas!

## Question and Answer Discussion

**James Bochnowski:** I'd like to direct this question to George. I'd like to hear the simple and blindingly obvious things we need to do to fix the economy. They're not so blindingly obvious to me.

**GS:** Number one: Reform the personal income and corporate tax system. The template is there from the 1986 Tax Act. People in the joint committee on taxation can score it overnight. Get the rate down and the junk out.

Do something of the same thing with the corporate tax rate. There's not enough junk to justify, on a revenue-neutral basis, getting the rate down as far as it should go, but get it down to something like 20 percent. Then say: this is the tax system, period. End of discussion.

Then you've got to do something about spending. What they're talking about now, which strikes me as ridiculous, is basically a trillion dollars here and a trillion dollars there ten years from now. The present Congress and president have no control whatever over what is spent ten years from now, so they backend load things. I say: ask not what a Congress ten years from now may spend; ask what you are going to spend this year and next year and get the line pointed downward.

Then there is the Congress. Congress has not done its work for at least three years. The Congress has the power of the purse, according to the Constitution, so it needs to exercise that power in a responsible way. And there's a clear way of doing it. Namely, the president proposes a budget. This year he didn't even propose a serious budget. Congress reviews it. They have a number. They pass it out. Committees hold hearings. They make informed judgments and appropriations and the result is a budget. For at least three years we've had continuing resolutions, a nonsensical way of doing the budget. Let's get back to normalcy and get the budget under control. It can be done.

Something has to be done about entitlements. Social Security is so simple. All you have to do is change from wage indexing to price indexing. I'd put John Shoven in charge of it. And if John and I had our way, we'd do another few wrinkles just to keep people in the labor force. For example, if you've paid into Social Security for forty years, you're totally paid in so there should be no more deductions. That means that you, an individual in your sixties, will have greater take-home pay and you won't cost the employer as much. We think that will keep people in the labor force longer, which will be a net plus.

In the medical area, there are many things that need to be done. Some things can be done administratively to get the consumer more involved in the game. For example, it is easily possible to use Medicare records to make publicly available prices and outcomes across the wide range of health providers. Then consumers can make intelligent choices. This can be done without revealing anybody's personal records. Then there are simple things like letting people buy insurance across state lines so there is competition among insurance providers. I think Paul Ryan has it fundamentally right: you want to convert the so-called entitlements under Medicare and Medicaid to the ability to buy health benefits. Let people have consumer power and, all of a sudden, you'll find that costs are brought under control.

That leaves the Federal Reserve. I hesitate to even say the words in the presence of Alan Greenspan, but I think the Fed should be careful, because if they don't get hold of themselves, they're going to get their wings clipped badly. They have the view, apparently, that they can do anything, that there are no limits. They can throw money at this and at that by the trillions of dollars. I think they should get back to the kind of monetary policy that Volcker and Greenspan conducted. It's more predictable. Now when anybody from the Fed makes a speech, people run around and say, "What are they going to do next?" Talk about uncertainty. This is a major addition to uncertainty. Show people that what the Fed is going to do is run a monetary policy consistent with prosperity without inflation; that's the Fed's job. A rules-based policy of some kind would probably be best. Try the Taylor Rule, for example, just to be parochial about it.

Put these things into place, announce that these are the economic policies, and then go on to something else. I think the economy would take off.

**David Henderson:** Question for Alan Greenspan. Alan, I like your proposal on H1-B but I just want a little more detail. When you say "get rid of it," what do you mean? Do you say—and I'm not objecting, I like it—that we'll allow three million people a year with certain qualifications? Ten million a year? That's great. Or are you saying something else? I'd just like to know what you're saying.

**AG:** I'd start off by being practical. Increase the quotas very significantly and keep increasing them. That avoids the question of the issue, which is a relevant question, about how you maintain the culture of a society if you're wide open to immigration. It's extremely difficult politically to keep that going, because of a tendency in any population group to try to freeze the nature of the group. But we cannot solve our skill problem without a very significant increase in the size of the quotas.

**Nicholas Hope:** At a conference across the road last year, Andrew Crockett offered the opinion that the combination of limited liability leverage and too-big-to-fail almost guaranteed that banks and other big financial institutions would make excessively risky bets. Now if we can agree that Dodd-Frank's not the answer, what would you recommend, Dr. Greenspan, as the changes we need in the financial regulation?

**AG:** Well, there's one particular change that was actually made in 1970, which in retrospect, was a mistake: that was the New York Stock Exchange ruling that enabled broker-dealers, who were required to be partnerships in 1970 and earlier, to incorporate. My recollection of broker-dealers, Goldman Sachs and Morgan Stanley at that time, is that they wouldn't lend you a dime overnight because partners were very, very tight with respect to doing anything. Had we had that type of culture and law throughout the last forty years, it would have been very difficult to create the types of problems that emerged with the financial bubbles that eventually got to the point where some of these investment banks had only 3 percent tangible capital. Back in the days when they were partnerships, they had more than adequate capital to the point, in many cases, where they behaved like many of the Swiss and German bankers who have said it is utterly unethical to ask a banker the size of his capital. One must presume it's more than adequate to cover anything you could conceive of. So I think that there's a major issue that we could solve if we worked our way back towards more personal legal responsibility to the individuals who were involved in these markets. I don't think you can regulate them in a manner that would prevent people from going around the regulation. These people are much too smart to get hung up with the specific regulation in the tax and regulatory codes. But if you create the changes at the base of the system, I grant you, you won't be able to raise as much capital as before, which is the reason they changed the 1970 ruling. But that's what you should have in mind.

**Robert Wilson:** I was impressed with your comments, Mr. Greenspan, with respect to improving our competitiveness through immigration laws. It seems to me that competitiveness is one of our basic issues, on a very broad front. I'd like to have the comments of the panel with respect to whether or not we need to regain competitiveness in order to build future growth in our economy.

**AG:** I'll start off by saying competitiveness is fundamental to a market system. Schumpeter's creative destruction is at the core of rising standards of living, and competition fosters that process. There is, as yet, little evidence, however, of any pronounced slowdown in productivity growth. But our demographics are sending ominous signals as we lose the most productive part of our workforce to retirement: the baby boomers.

**GS:** This is also an opportunity to underscore the importance of vastly improving the job we're doing with K–12 education. If we wind up with a large group of people in this country who don't have the educational attainments they need to do the kind of work that's there, we're in deep trouble.

**AG:** We already are in deep trouble.

**GS:** Yes, we are.

**JC:** I would like to add a caution against using that word, "competitiveness." Most people who use it think that we're in a race with China, to "compete" and export to them more than they export to us. That's a classic economic fallacy. Competition is great. But the objective of our society is to grow and become prosperous, not to compete with China for who can send more cars the other way in exchange for more useless pieces of paper. Economics is not a zero sum game.

GS: There were some fascinating charts shown on savings this morning. Households in this country are starting to save again. Everybody's beating on them to stop but they have started to save again and they're only spending something like 96 percent of their income. But the big problem in government is the giant rate of dis-saving. Somehow, as part of this balance, we've got to get savings in tune with our investment. Then we won't have to import savings from China and the trade account will balance itself out. I recommend that you read a very interesting article written by Ron McKinnon for the Summer 2010 publication of the *SIEPR Policy Brief*.[5] It lays this out in the clearest way you can imagine.

**William Hume:** Is there a point at which government becomes sufficiently large that it crowds out the private sector and stifles any ability of the private sector to develop competition and to compete?

GS: Well, obviously you can get so big, taking such a large share of GDP, that you have to support it with taxation. That automatically is pulling the rug out from under the private sector. There are essential functions that government has to do, and we should want the government to do them well. We need to be a lawful society or it won't work. We need to be able to defend ourselves and conduct a reasonable foreign policy. We probably need to have some transfer programs, but we need to structure them to work well so that users have the ability to utilize the competitive structure of the economy to keep costs under control. So I would say yes to your

---

5. Ronald McKinnon, "Why Exchange Rates Will Not Correct Global Trade Imbalances," *SIEPR Policy Brief*, June 2010, Stanford University.

question, but I would also say that government has vital functions to perform and we want them performed well. It is possible.

JC: May I add, "yes," and one of the signs is when government stops going beyond those vital functions and wants to run the economy, tell us what kind of cars to drive, and all of the rest of it. This morning we got rid of the fallacy that you just have to watch the taxes. You have to watch the spending because those are the future taxes. But even spending isn't everything. If the government says, "You shall buy a different kind of car," that's the same thing as taxing and spending just by another means. Governments can really screw things up when they're telling everybody what to do, deciding which companies fail and which will survive. But none of that shows up as on-budget taxes or spending.

GS: I have to say that I have solar panels on my house here on campus and I'm driving an all-electric car. So I say, "Take that, Ahmadinejad!"

John Bourgoin: Is there a set of policies the government could put in place that would bring back the relatively low-wage manufacturing jobs for the large mass of people who aren't well-educated and aren't likely to be well-educated?

AG: I'll respond to that. You know, I often wonder about the premise of the question. One of the things that this country has done, and indeed, that all of the cutting-edge-oriented countries have done, is move away from the physical substance of manufacturing and move towards increasingly conceptual, more valuable ideas. And it's not an accident that we've had a dramatic decline in manufacturing in the United States, because, leaving aside the import/export issues, consumers within the United States, acting voluntarily, to the extent that they can, are choosing these ephemeral things. I'm not only talking about choosing services over physical goods, but within the scope of technically manufactured goods, they're downsizing to the point where they're doing more and more computer-based hardware, for example, or anything based on silicon chips, and going forward from there. I wonder whether we want to revert back to the technology of the nineteenth century. Steel, for example, is a fairly labor-intensive industry, especially in the rolling mill operations—there's a technology that can employ an awful lot of people. But it's nineteenth-century technology. You cannot increase standards of living by going in that direction. So we have to be careful in trying to replicate every labor-intensive output, because by definition, labor-intensive output necessarily means low productivity.

And so I seriously question whether we should be seeking jobs in that particular area. In fact, the Chinese are doing precisely that. They are keeping their exchange rate abnormally low and in the process, creating a demand abroad for low-quality goods embodying very substantial amounts of labor input. One of the reasons why they are very strongly opposed to allowing their exchange rate to rise is that it would increase the quality of what is required to be exported from China at a profit. That means, essentially, you'd have to use a lot more equipment to produce the goods they ship out than they are currently using today. A higher exchange rate will force them, in order to maintain higher profit charges, to shift to more equipment and less labor. The result of this is that we can get a higher level of employment in the United States by working backwards, going to lower technologies and lower standards of living. I don't think that is an alternative we should wish to pursue.

**GS:** Let me just add that if you keep raising the minimum wage, at a certain point you'll price these people you're worried about out of the market. Why do we want to do that? I think it's much better to have them working than on welfare of some kind. I think the minimum wage is part of it, but let me just make a comment on a favorite hobby horse of mine that I never seem to get anywhere with.

Our national accounts were created by some very smart guys at the National Bureau of Economic Research back in the 1920s and '30s. The accounts are the same now as they were then but our economy bears no resemblance to what it was then. Time goes on and new jobs appear. Where do we slot them into this set of categories? Sometimes there's an easy way; sometimes it's hard. If you're really frustrated in finding the right category, you call the job a service, so after a while we become a service economy. Everyone thinks of that as flipping hamburgers and doing laundry, but a lot of other new, productive things get classified as services. I think it's long past time that Jim Poterba, the new head of the National Bureau, undertake a review of how to describe our economy more accurately today. That would be better, I believe, than slotting new things into old categories that are getting more and more obsolete.

**Clarke Swanson:** I wonder, if in retrospect, that you can consider the repeal of Glass-Steagall to have been a wise move?

**AG:** It was an exceptionally wise move and, in fact, when the actual repeal occurred, it was redundant. In the early part of

1987 there was a court ruling which enabled an interpretation of Glass-Steagall to include a loophole for what they called Section 20 affiliates of bank holding companies—which essentially were investment banks. The Section 20 affiliates became ubiquitous. Everyone had them. So the actual repeal of Glass-Steagall in 2000 had no impact whatsoever. The 2000 legislation, Gramm-Leach-Bliley, set up financial services holding companies. But nobody applied for a charter because everybody who wanted to be in both the commercial and investment banking business had already done so through the Section 20 affiliates. The only thing the Gramm-Leach-Bliley Act did was to lower the cost of some of the redundant requirements for Section 20 affiliates. Glass-Steagall was originally enacted in 1933, and was different from what we really thought it was, according to the 1987 court ruling.

GS: But at the same time—and these guys know a lot more about the subject than I do—it seems to me that when you have organizations that have deposits insured, access to the Fed's discount window, and all sorts of special privileges like that, it's not unreasonable to say: you can't indulge in super-risky trading activities.

AG: I actually agree with that, George.

GS: Why, thank you!

AG: The basic problem is not in the structure, it's in the subsidies that are coming from government. What you're basically saying is that government subsidies should not be used in a manner other than what their purpose is. There's no way to get deposit insurance without creating a moral hazard. The only question is: what is the trade-off? And I know that all the evidence suggests that runs on banks stopped cold with the introduction of deposit insurance. But it has had other adverse consequences. You cannot have a system which grants unlimited entitlement, which is basically what deposit insurance is, without consequences.

**GS:** Well, let's leave it at this: all is not well in the financial industry.

## Discussion Commentators

| | |
|---|---|
| **James J. Bochnowski** | General partner, Delphi Ventures and Hoover overseer |
| **David Henderson** | Hoover research fellow, Hoover Institution, Stanford University |
| **Nicholas Hope** | Director, Stanford Center for International Development, Stanford University |
| **William J. Hume** | Chairman, Basic American, Inc. and Hoover overseer |
| **W. Clarke Swanson Jr.** | Owner, Swanson Vineyards & Winery and Hoover overseer |
| **Robert C. Wilson** | Former vice president General Electric, executive vice president Rockwell International, CEO Collins Radio and CEO Memorex |

# CHAPTER 9

# Summary of the Commentary

IAN J. WRIGHT

Chapters 2 through 7 of this book grew out of presentations given at the conference on "Restoring Robust Economic Growth in America" at Hoover Institution, Stanford University, on December 2, 2011. Questions and comments from the audience to the authors followed the presentations. This chapter is a summary of the discussion that occurred, grouped broadly according to whether it pertained to presentations on activism and policy uncertainty or monetary and fiscal policy.

## Activism and Policy Uncertainty

**Robert Hall** commented that he would characterize the investment puzzle discussed by Alan Greenspan as there being strong corporate cash flow and a low cost of capital but very weak total investment. Hall explained recent work he had done looking at both the household side, including residential investment and all categories of consumption, as well as the business side, essentially plant, equipment, and inventory investment. In this work he said he sorted out cross effects between business and residential components and showed that declining consumption demand automatically reduces investment because, he argued, there is no reason to invest if people aren't buying enough "stuff," which he said is the main problem with the U.S. economy. He claimed that were people consuming more, plant and equipment investment would be closer to target, and that much of the effect on expenditure of the crisis actually came through the household.

Hall also argued that macro models had, in fact, incorporated crisis effects and that many papers are actually trying to describe the current post-crisis U.S. economy, although he recognized that some researchers have used government multipliers derived from pre-crisis models and applied them in the crisis. Hall said that government purchases have declined relative to trends continuously throughout the crisis and have become a considerable drag, and that the rise in the government spending multiplier near the zero interest rate lower bound has worsened the drag since government expenditures are contracting.

**Alan Greenspan** responded to Hall's comments by saying that he would need to see exactly how Hall related plant and equipment investment to the rest of the consumption and investment system to be able to comment precisely on Hall's explanation, but argued that the way capital investment is made is, in fact, as he modeled it in his presentation. Greenspan said profit margins have been opening up in general and that the share of profit and cash flow relative to GDP has been rising so that other elements of GDP are not as relevant if one can explain capital investment strictly from cash flow. Greenspan further argued that capital investment is not made based on what GDP aggregates are via regression, but that it's made via a decision process as he modeled it in his presentation.

Greenspan also discussed crowding out in response to Hall's comment and said what has been crowded out has not been showing up in the AAA or BBB credits, but in the DDD+ and CCC credits, where interest rates are 10–15 percent, so arguments that crowding out is occurring on companies with low interest rates and highly-rated securities are not relevant.

Adding to the discussion of Greenspan's presentation, **Michael Boskin** said multipliers such as those referred to by Hall can decline rapidly and can even turn negative if substantial taxes and spending are expected beyond the zero interest rate lower bound period, which has been the case in 2009–2010 due to the large deficits which are unlikely to be paid back until well into the future. He warned that it is important researchers keep in mind that deficits are not created in a vacuum and expectations of future spending and taxes can put downward pressure on the sizes of multipliers relative to what is being estimated, and that expectations of spending and taxes may not always be taken into account in models.

**Myron Scholes** voiced his agreement with the ideas on uncertainty and how they were presented by Greenspan. He asked Greenspan to what extent he believed attacking the housing problem in the U.S. would reduce uncertainty and thereby stimulate economic growth, and also asked Greenspan what suggestions he had for resolving the housing problem. Greenspan responded by saying housing has turned out to be a disproportionally critical aspect of the slow recovery. He argued that housing prices are the key driver of people's investment in housing and that a stabilization of home prices will lead to higher levels of owner occupancy. He noted that the current occupancy rate is well below its peak

and has returned to where it was in 1998. Greenspan said a restoration of home price stability will come as a more speculative
component of housing demand comes back and stated that housing prices can be extremely ambiguous and distorted due to two
separate streams of housing sales: normal and distressed. Thus, he
argued, to restore house price stability we must run out of distressed sales. To accomplish this, Greenspan recommended a
selling climax of houses which would cause all sellers to leave the
market. He claimed that a series of smaller selling climaxes has
led to the slow recovery and that the one market in this economy
which has not been controlled by government, the stock market,
is the one that has behaved the best because a large selling climax
occurred and then the market began to turn around. In other markets, policy has not allowed a large selling climax to occur and has
instead prolonged the recovery.

Commenting on the presentation of Scott Baker, Steven Davis
and Nick Bloom, **Joe Haubrich** said that it seemed the presenters
were referring to Knightian uncertainty as their measure of uncertainty, noted that this measure of uncertainty has been shown to
have different consequences for people's behavior than other measures of risk, and asked the presenters for their comments on this.
**Steven Davis** responded that the way to interpret their index is
not entirely clear and so it is difficult to say what it means for how
people will behave. He said that he and his coauthors used the
same methodology employed in creating their index to create a
financial uncertainty index and that it seemed to move very closely
with the VIX, a measure of market assessments of future volatility in equity returns, but that beyond this they cannot make any
definitive statement to Haubrich's point. Davis also commented
that part of what he and his coauthors see themselves doing is con-

structing a measure of economic uncertainty that will serve as an input into different economic models, some of which emphasize risk and some of which emphasize Knightian uncertainty, to help address the open question of how individuals respond to different types of uncertainty.

**Myron Scholes** inquired further about the uncertainty index relative to the VIX, noting the VIX is a forward measure of uncertainty over a period of time while the methodology the authors presented develops a daily index, and asked how the two indices compare due to this difference. Davis said he and his coauthors constructed a monthly financial uncertainty index using newspaper mentions satisfying their criteria within a month and then compared this with the VIX over that same month, as the VIX is a measure of expected market volatility over the next thirty days. He noted that they have not tried to do something more refined such as isolating newspaper articles talking about financial uncertainty in a forward-looking way, so to what extent the index they constructed is reacting to the VIX or trying to anticipate what might be happening is unclear from what they have done so far. However, Davis said, the fact that the application of their news-based approach to an index of equity market volatility behaves very similar to the VIX is reassuring, and indicates that the approach captures actual developments in the economy.

**Michael Boskin** asked Baker, Bloom, and Davis how they would differentiate between "types" of uncertainty after positing a scenario where the index gave the same level of uncertainty, but the type of uncertainty was different. He asked if they had thought about how to understand what the nature of the uncertainty their index is measuring is, and whether it might comport with what economists think are better or worse "types" of uncertainty. Davis responded that many macroeconomic models will imply that both first and second moment aspects of economic policy should matter and that he and his coauthors agree with this view. He stated that much more progress has been made professionally in measuring the first moment aspect than the second moment aspect, and so they are trying to add some measurements on the second moment, in addition to the more standard first moment measures already existing. Davis explained this could be done in two ways. The first is to more carefully dissect the nature of the news articles and he explained this is something he and his coauthors should do more of, although they have done some. The second is to try to control statistically for, or directly include measures of first moment effects, which he said they have done using the vector auto-regression (VAR)-based projections of future employment and industrial production.[1]

**Ronald McKinnon** commented that the financial index presented did not appear to include news on exchange rates, which would be pertinent, and encouraged Baker, Bloom, and Davis to consider this. In response, Davis suggested that he and his coauthors rename their financial uncertainty index the "index of equity market uncertainty," since they used terms such as "stock markets" and "equity returns" to determine the pertinent news articles. He also stated that exchange rate/currency issues were measured with more refinement when they decomposed their economic policy uncertainty index into different categories, although he agreed there is scope for further refinement.

**John Taylor** said that the policy uncertainty index appeared to represent policy which is itself more discretionary and less predict-

---

1. See Figure 3 in Chapter 3 of this volume for details.

able. As an example he noted that the huge amount of speculation about what the next step will be in the United States is probably why the monetary policy index rises so significantly. Taylor asked Baker, Bloom, and Davis if they agreed with this and if they could preview what their longer historical work in the 1970s will be since the 1970s was another period which was somewhat discretionary as well. Davis responded by arguing that there's no current strategy for the conduct of policy and conjectured that evidence of this is seen in the big swings in the stock market from 2008 forward. He observed that a disproportionate share of the large swings in the equity markets in the past few years reflects policy developments as they show up in the news, which supports Taylor's remarks. With regard to the 1970s, Davis noted that their preliminary work shows some increase in the index of economic policy uncertainty in the 1970s relative to the 1950s and 1960s. He also said that they see even larger movements in the 1930s, not surprisingly. However, Davis explained that he and his coauthors are still determining how to most appropriately scale the index to account for temporal differences in how news is reported.

Pertaining to the VARs, **Pete Klenow** asked how Baker, Bloom, and Davis disentangle whether policy uncertainty is causing shocks or responding to them. Davis explained the Cholesky ordering that they are using and that the impulse-response functions are not very sensitive to the particular ordering they choose. He said that this doesn't fully address the identification issue though because the policy uncertainty index could be responding to the anticipations of future developments, and so he and his coauthors are cautious in their interpretation. Davis believes they can say with some confidence that, conditional on current lag values of output, employment, investment, stock market performance, and so on, an innovation in their policy uncertainty index foreshadows substantial declines in investment, output, and employment over the next two years. **Nicholas Bloom** added that their view is that bad economic circumstances generate policy uncertainty. The question is if any additional causal effect exists from policy uncertainty, and their sense is probably yes. Bloom explained that measuring that effect is hard and that you can see the policy uncertainty index as an amplification mechanism: it didn't cause the initial recession, but it's maybe made it worse. Davis said they do have a long-run strategy for trying to identify the causal effect of policy uncertainty on economic outcomes, which is to use the timing and the closeness of national elections as an instrument for identifying the effects of policy uncertainty on macroeconomic outcomes.

**Michael Bordo** asked how the index changes when different newspaper key words such as "crisis," "inflation," "deflation," and "depression" are used in place of the current ones that are used to create the policy uncertainty index, and explained this could shed further light on the direction of causality. Davis explained that he and his coauthors have done a fair amount of tweaking of the key words used to determine the index in the 1985–2011 period using the Google News–based index but that they've only very recently started pushing back to 1900 and are still in the early stages. Bloom explained that they have also done some checks with the VARs to see if their measure of uncertainty was just a proxy for bad news but that it doesn't appear to be at first glance.

**Robert Hall** returned to Boskin's point that some events might be recorded as an increase in uncertainty in the index even though they are first moment effects, due to their significant discussion in the press, and argues this may bias the results against revealing the unique effect of the second moment. He inquired if there was a way around this. In response Davis reiterated the two approaches he explained to Boskin and noted he sees value in both approaches.

A member of the audience shared his feeling that there's been a difference in journalism through time. He explained that in 1970 media bias may not be found to as strong a degree as it is today since in an earlier period of journalism there was very little editorial content relative to factual reporting but that now this may be different. He therefore asked Baker, Bloom, and Davis if they are making adjustments to account for this through time. Davis agreed it is an important issue and affects the theory used as to how the index is constructed and what one thinks the index accomplishes. He outlined two views which suggest two somewhat different approaches to constructing their news-based indices. The first is that each particular news source provides a noisy signal of the true underlying economic reality, which leads to a sampling problem: one obtains many noisy, possibly even biased signals of the truth, and then applies standard statistical sampling methods to infer the truth. The second is that the news media either unintentionally or deliberately influence business people's perceptions, and those perceptions in turn affect the economy. He explained that the second approach pushes one to give more weight to more important news sources by some measure of their influence and that for this purpose he and his coauthors plan to use data on subscription counts for print newspapers, and unique daily page visits for online news sources. Davis also expressed the view that he and his coauthors should go down both paths he outlined: one in which they interpret news sources as noisy signals of the truth, and another in which they interpret them as influencing perceptions, which in turn influence economic activity.

## Monetary and Fiscal Policy

Commenting on Robert Hall's presentation, **Ronald McKinnon** argued that while it is very conventional to relate consumer spending to the real interest rate, and numerous economists want increased inflation to drive the real interest rate down, announcing a policy of increasing inflation would introduce a great deal of uncertainty since the Fed has very little control over what the effect of such a policy announcement would be. **Robert Hall** responded by saying he doesn't advocate the creation of inflation but suggested that economists need to send a signal to consumers that what they would normally get through a low interest rate they can get through some other mechanisms.

McKinnon then argued that if the nominal interest rate goes to zero then the whole system of bank intermediation is disrupted since as interest rates approach zero, the interbank market stops functioning. He cited as evidence the state of the banking system currently, with large banks not lending their excess reserves to small banks. Hall responded by claiming interest rates are continuous down to the negative domain and argued that since interest rates are just a relative price of today versus one period from now, there is no reason why that relative price can't be less than one, which is an interest rate that's negative. Hence, negative interest rates should not disrupt the banking system.

McKinnon then commented on Hall's new proposals. He agreed that phasing in something like a value-added tax and announcing in advance that this policy would be phased in would encourage consumers to spend today and, in effect, show them a lower interest rate so they would spend more today and that this would have a positive effect on the economy. McKinnon then stated that breaking the link between deposits/reserves and currencies would be too extreme a proposal and did not think it a good idea. Hall agreed the latter may in fact be a little too extreme but noted it's a good thing to think about new options and ideas.

**Steven Davis** asked Hall whether he was concerned that his proposed policies would encourage households to save less in a period when household balance sheets are already somewhat precarious, and that the effect of this reduction in savings would make them more precarious and make households more vulnerable to huge economic shocks. Hall responded that most of the positive effect on the economy he would imagine as coming from those households that are unconstrained and able to spend more, noting 42 percent of consumption occurs in unconstrained households. Davis commented that these policies might bring unconstrained households closer to being constrained by inducing them to save less and thereby make them more susceptible to shocks. To this Hall explained that unconstrained individuals are generally older, have liquid assets, and can draw down on their liquid assets to buy durables and other goods now that they were going to buy in the future, and thus remain unconstrained. Hall also noted that business investment is always unconstrained, and with lower interest rates businesses would invest, spend and hire more since resources are cheap and unemployment is high.

Davis accepted that lowering the real interest rate has benefits but asked Hall to point to a previous time in history in which there was a previous housing bust or financial crisis of the magnitude just experienced that was followed by a monetary authority successfully pursuing Hall's interest rate strategy to get the economy back on track. Hall responded that a 1993 paper by Christina Romer states the hypothesis that the very rapid expansion of real

GDP that occurred in the recovery from 1933 to 1937 and then from 1938 into WWII (roughly 10 percent annual GDP growth rates) was such a case. He explained that real interest rates fell to minus 12 percent in the middle of 1941 and that this was followed by a huge increase in output, noting however that the question of how that relates to the mobilization that was getting started due to WWII is important as well.

**Michael Bordo** said another proposal to increase spending put forth in the 1930s by Silvio Gesell was to issue notes taxed at a certain rate each month so people spend their money quickly. Hall noted that numerous similarly unique proposals were made and some were implemented during the 1929 and 1933 deflation.

**John Cochrane** said he was not persuaded of Hall's arguments. He argued the zero bound on the short term Federal Funds rate might not really be the central wedge or distortion in the economy right now, especially relative to the large distortions in the labor market or the uncertainty effects described by Steven Davis. He noted that the Taylor Rule may give guidance as to the right policy but that it is a linear regression: It describes past Fed behavior well, but is neither an optimal rule, nor does it make much sense to extrapolate it to unknown territory of negative interest rates. Cochrane then asked Hall whether he really believed the marginal product of capital was negative, requiring negative real interest rates, and why policy should counteract the average American's desire to save and invest rather than consume. He noted that the common deflationary spiral story, that deflation and a zero nominal rate mean high real rates, does not apply: We still have positive inflation, so real rates are already about negative three percent. How much more negative do real rates need to be? He also noted that the "zero bound" refers to short-term treasury bills. In fact, companies are paying closer to 6 percent interest. So the zero bound is not binding on the interest rates that actually clear the market for corporate capital.

Hall responded by agreeing that the Taylor Rule may not come up with the right number in terms of the effect that an interest rate change would have on output, but that he still believes that if unemployment is high then the Fed can lower it by lowering the interest rate, even if that means making interest rates negative. He argued that once monetary policy is liberated so it can generate negative interest rates the Fed will have sufficient power to do monetary policy to help the economy. Hall also made the argument that rates move together and so if the Federal Funds rate changed, all rates would follow it and noted that some are already negative so having negative rates is not impossible.

Hall also said the fundamental wedge in the economy is the gap between the low marginal value of time of people who are unemployed and the marginal product of labor, which remains more or less at its normal level, and that the policies he proposed will close this gap. Cochrane said both he and Davis have been trying to point out that the fundamental problem is a micro problem and, in addition, that labor economists will argue that unemployment could be due to mismatches or a host of other issues that lowering interest rates won't necessarily fix. Hall responded that mismatches and these other issues are small contributors to a much larger overall unemployment level.

**Michael Boskin** commented that a lot of discussion has occurred about dealing with the short run and what the long-run ramifications are, and said this gets back to the question of whether Hall can successfully implement these short-run policies without causing problems in the long run, noting people's expectations about the long-run affect the short run.

**George Siguler** pointed out that a consistent view at the conference seemed to have been that there are huge problems in unemployment and government policy, but that there has been less talk about problems in the corporate sector even though many economic problems are likely to occur in that sector over the next few years. He said the real estate industry needs a huge infusion of equity to have a reasonable balance sheet as an industry, which would cause many to consider it a primary problem, but pointed out that it is not really being discussed at the conference even though it is quite a large, lingering problem. Hall responded that although real estate was left out of his discussion, it is because it is a big sector in terms of value, but not in terms of expenditure relative to GDP. Thus, it is a less important sector for the discussion at hand, although he agreed a completely correct analysis would also need to factor in the leveraged, non-household sector of commercial real estate.

Discussing John Cogan and John Taylor's presentation, **Myron Scholes** asked whether the reduction in net borrowing could be because states can't borrow due to market conditions of the time, but still have to pay down old debt and so they are forced to use ARRA money in this way. **John Taylor** responded by noting the large increase in state-held assets and argued that even if states were borrowing constrained, the reason why net borrowing declined is due to states increasing their holdings of financial assets. Although Taylor also said that to fully answer Scholes's question, one would need to look at disaggregated state and local data and which governments were constrained, which he said he and Cogan plan to do. Scholes said states could be essentially defeasing their debt over time with securities bought with stimulus funds, to which Taylor agreed. Taylor also gave two additional interpretations of the results. The first was that states' behavior with ARRA stimulus funds is similar to consumer behavior under permanent income theory: when consumers get temporary funds they save them. States knew ARRA funds were temporary and so they saved them with a plan to gradually use them over time. The second was that the results show that the federal government borrowed more, the state and local governments borrowed less, and the household sector borrowed less.

**Steven Davis** commented that the claim the ARRA actually reduced purchases by state and local governments was striking. He asked whether it's possible to test this claim empirically by exploiting state variation in the extent to which "hold-harmless" provisions referenced in the presentation bind. Taylor answered that he and Cogan have not yet done tests of the nature Davis suggested, although he thought it a good idea to do so, explaining the state-level data required to do such tests is not as clean as the national data, so constructing such tests is difficult. Taylor stated that they did do a test using the aggregate data by removing the portions of ARRA stimulus explicitly allocated for Medicaid payments and checking if doing this changed coefficient estimates in their regression, which it didn't. He explained they are still looking for empirical evidence verifying their claim.

**Michael Boskin** noted Taylor originally presented his results with a more modern new Keynesian model and some modest impact multipliers in the short run that turn negative eventually, and that Taylor's data indicated federal purchases were very trivial during the time of the ARRA and that states didn't make purchases either so the size of the government multipliers would be less important. He asked if, as a result, one should conclude that Taylor's results for ARRA are generalizable, and, in addition, if the government might be able to figure out some way to construct a different, more effective stimulus package. Taylor responded that his and Cogan's work is not informative in the debate about the size of the government multiplier, but shows that since government purchases were small that debate should matter less. He also doubted whether differently constructed federal stimulus packages to the states would have increased state purchases since states are likely to continue to fund current projects rather than begin new ones. Taylor did suggest that if more "shovel-ready" projects were had at the state level then perhaps such packages could work. Boskin commented that infrastructure has changed such that "shovels" are no longer used since most public projects use massive equipment and are far less labor intensive than in the Great Depression.

Boskin also asked whether motivating the use of stimulus funds to speed up purchases that would be made later anyway (such as military equipment) could be done in an effective way. Taylor explained the process of "speeding up" the purchase of goods may sound good but is not as simple as pressing a button, even in the case of defense goods. He added that even if it was done he doubted it would have made a large difference in stimulating the economy.

**Myron Scholes** asked whether studying the stimulus package of China might lend insight into whether federal stimulus made to local governments can be done in a different, more effective way. He explained that China did its stimulus by making loans through the banking system to local governments and that there might be records of the explicit purposes of the loans. Taylor responded that he and Cogan began a cross-country comparison but that it has been a slow process to complete as the Chinese data are less transparent relative to that of the United States.

**Pete Klenow** asked whether the increased transfers, including Medicaid, at the state level have been concentrated in liquidity-constrained households and, therefore, have boosted private consumption. Taylor answered that their current study is focused on government purchases rather than private consumption, since most of the political and academic debate has taken place with regard to those, but that he had done previous work showing the permanent income model for households seems to explain household behavior with stimulus funds well: since 2000, stimulus checks sent to individuals appear to have had very little impact on aggregate consumption data. Taylor explained that this doesn't mean liquidity-constrained individuals aren't spending the money, but does mean that effect is not showing up in the aggregate data. Pertaining to Medicaid, Taylor shared his belief that he doesn't think the *impact* of Medicaid payments has been different from the impact of other payments, although he conceded that Medicaid is a different *type* of payment.

## Discussion Commentators

| | |
|---|---|
| **Michael Bordo** | Professor of economics and director of the Center for Monetary and Financial History at Rutgers University; national fellow at Hoover Institution, Stanford University |

| | |
|---|---|
| **Michael Boskin** | Senior fellow at Hoover Institution and T. M. Friedman Professor of Economics, Stanford University |
| **Joseph G. Haubrich** | Vice president and economist, Federal Reserve Bank of Cleveland |
| **Pete Klenow** | Professor of economics, Stanford University |
| **Ronald McKinnon** | William D. Eberle Professor of International Economics, emeritus, Stanford University |
| **Myron Scholes** | Frank E. Buck Professor of Finance, emeritus, Stanford University Graduate School of Business and chairman, Platinum Grove Asset Management, L.P. |
| **George W. Siguler** | Managing director, Siguler Guff & Company and Hoover overseer |

# About the Authors

**Scott R. Baker** is a fourth-year PhD candidate in the Department of Economics at Stanford University. His research is concentrated on empirical labor and public economics, especially in the area of federal policy analysis and evaluation. He is currently engaged in a variety of empirical research projects regarding the effects of uncertainty on growth, the relationship between immigration policy and crime, as well as the effects of unemployment benefits on job-search intensity. Baker was born and raised in San Diego, California, and received BAs in 2007 in economics and political science from the University of California, Berkeley, where he was awarded the Earl Rolph Memorial Prize. He is also a consultant for Intuit, working with their Advanced Data Sciences team to leverage small business data for market research and to design forecasting algorithms.

**Nicholas Bloom** is a professor in the Department of Economics and a courtesy professor in the Graduate School of Business at Stanford University. He is the codirector of the Productivity Program at the National Bureau of Economic Research. His main research interests are measuring and explaining management and organizational practices across firms and countries, and the causes and consequences of uncertainty arising from events such as the

9/11 terrorist attack and the recent credit crunch. Bloom previously worked in London, England, as a tax policy adviser at HM Treasury under Gordon Brown, and as a management consultant at McKinsey & Company. In 2008 he won an Alfred Sloan Fellowship and an NSF Career Award, and in 2009 the Frisch Medal from the Econometric Society.

**JOHN H. COCHRANE** is the AQR Capital Management Distinguished Service Professor of Finance at the University of Chicago Booth School of Business, a research associate of the National Bureau of Economic Research, and an adjunct scholar of the CATO Institute. He is a past president of the American Finance Association. Cochrane earned a bachelor's degree in physics at the Massachusetts Institute of Technology and a PhD in economics at the University of California, Berkeley. He is the author of academic articles on risk and liquidity premiums in stock and bond markets, the volatility of exchange rates, the term structure of interest rates, the returns to venture capital, the relation between stock prices and investment, option pricing, the relationship between deficits and inflation, the effects of monetary policy, health insurance, time-series econometrics, and other topics. He is the author of the popular textbook *Asset Pricing* and a coauthor of *The Squam Lake Report*. He also writes occasional op-eds for the *Wall Street Journal* and other publications, and blogs as "the Grumpy Economist."

**JOHN F. COGAN** is the Leonard and Shirley Ely Senior Fellow at the Hoover Institution and a professor in the Public Policy Program at Stanford University. He is a former deputy director of the U.S. Office of Management and Budget. His current research focuses on U.S. budget and fiscal policy, social security, and health care policy. His most recent book, coauthored with Hoover fellow Daniel Kessler and Glenn Hubbard, is *Healthy, Wealthy, and Wise: Five Steps to a Better Health Care System*. Cogan currently serves on faculty advisory boards for the Stanford-in-Washington campus and the Stanford Institute for Economic Policy Research. He received Stanford-in-Government's Distinguished Service Award in 1994. He serves on Hoover's Working Group on Health Care Policy, the Working Group on Economic Policy, and the Shultz-Stephenson Task Force on Energy Policy. He is on the board of directors of Gilead Sciences and Venture Lending and Leasing, and also on the board of trustees of the Charles Schwab Family of Funds and Sacred Heart Schools in Atherton, California. Cogan received his AB in 1969 and his PhD in 1976 from the University of California, Los Angeles, both in economics.

**STEVEN J. DAVIS** is the William H. Abbott Professor of International Business and Economics at the University of Chicago Booth School of Business and former editor of the *American Economic Journal: Macroeconomics*. He is also a research associate with the National Bureau of Economic Research, an economic adviser to the U.S. Congressional Budget Office, a visiting scholar at the Federal Reserve Bank of Chicago, and a visiting scholar at the American Enterprise Institute. Previously, he held positions at the Hoover Institution at Stanford University, the Massachusetts Institute of Technology, the National University of Singapore, and Charles River Associates. Davis earned a bachelor's degree in 1980 from Portland State University and MA and PhD degrees in 1981 and 1986 from Brown University, all in economics. His research interests include employment and wage behavior, business dynamics, national economic performance, and economic fluctuations.

**ALAN GREENSPAN** served as chairman of the Federal Reserve Board for eighteen-and-a-half years, and earlier (1974–77) as chairman of President Ford's Council of Economic Advisers. From 1981 to 1983, he served as chairman of the National Commission on Social Security Reform. Before his appointment to the Fed in 1987, Greenspan served as a director of J. P. Morgan, Mobil, Alcoa, General Foods, and Capital Cities/ABC. He has received the Legion of Honor from France (commander), became an honorary knight commander of the British Empire, and received the Medal of Freedom, the United States' highest civil award. He currently heads Greenspan Associates and is the author of *The Age of Turbulence*. Greenspan is married to Andrea Mitchell, NBC's chief foreign affairs correspondent and host of MSNBC's *Andrea Mitchell Reports*.

**ROBERT E. HALL** is the Robert and Carole McNeil Joint Professor of Economics at Stanford University and a senior fellow at the Hoover Institution. His research focuses on the overall performance of the U.S. economy, including unemployment, capital formation, financial activity, and inflation. He has served as president, vice president, and Ely Lecturer of the American Economic Association and is a distinguished fellow of the association. He is an elected member of the National Academy of Sciences and a fellow of the American Academy of Arts and Sciences, the Society of Labor Economists, and the Econometric Society. He is director of the Research Program on Economic Fluctuations and Growth of the National Bureau of Economic

Research. He was a member of the National Presidential Advisory Committee on Productivity.

**KYLE F. HERKENHOFF** is a fourth-year PhD candidate at the University of California, Los Angeles, Department of Economics. As an intern at the Research Department of the Federal Reserve Bank of St. Louis, he is currently involved in several projects that look at the aggregate employment implications of mortgage modifications and foreclosure delays, how the aging workforce changes the nature of recoveries, and the effect of intellectual property laws on growth. He is a visiting scholar at the Office of the Chief Economist of the United States Patent and Trademark Office and a recipient of the Richard Ziman Research Fellowship. He grew up overseas in Indonesia and Australia and, upon returning to the United States, completed his bachelor's degree in economics and mathematics at the University of California, Los Angeles.

**ELLEN R. MCGRATTAN** is a monetary advisor at the Federal Reserve Bank of Minneapolis and an adjunct professor of economics at the University of Minnesota. She is also a fellow for the Society for the Advancement of Economic Theory, a research economist at the National Bureau of Economic Research, an editor at the *Review of Economic Dynamics,* a member of the Bureau of Economic Analysis Advisory Committee, and a past member of the American Economic Association Executive Committee. McGrattan received her BS in mathematics and economics from Boston College and a PhD in economics from Stanford University. Her research is concerned with the aggregate effects of monetary and fiscal policy—in particular, the effects on GDP, investment, the allocation of hours, and the stock market.

**LEE E. OHANIAN** is a professor of economics and director of the Ettinger Family Program in Macroeconomic Research at the University of California, Los Angeles, where he has taught since 1999, and a senior fellow at the Hoover Institution. He is also associate director of the Center for the Advanced Study in Economic Efficiency at Arizona State University. He is an adviser to the Federal Reserve Bank of Minneapolis and has previously advised other Federal Reserve banks, foreign central banks, and the National Science Foundation. Ohanian's research, which focuses on economic crises, has been published widely in a number of peer-reviewed journals. He previously served on the faculties of the Universities of Minnesota and Pennsylvania and has been a visiting professor at the Stockholm School of Economics, Arizona State, and the University of Southern California. He is codirector of the research initiative "Macroeconomics across Time and Space" at the National Bureau of Economic Research. Ohanian received a BA in economics from the University of California, Santa Barbara, and an MA and a PhD in economics from the University of Rochester.

**EDWARD C. PRESCOTT** is the W. P. Carey Chaired Professor of Economics and the director of the Center for the Advanced Study in Economic Efficiency at Arizona State University. He is also a senior monetary adviser at the Federal Reserve Bank of Minneapolis. In 2004, he was awarded the Nobel Prize in Economic Sciences jointly with Finn Kydland for their contributions to dynamic macroeconomics, in particular, the time consistency of economic policy and the driving forces behind business cycles. In addition, Prescott was awarded the 2002 Erwin Plein Nemmers Prize in Economics, elected a fellow of the American Academy of Arts and Sciences (1992) and a fellow of the Econometrica Society (1980), and selected to be a Guggenheim fellow (1974–75). In 2008, he was elected a member of the National Academy of Science. He received a BA in mathematics from Swarthmore College, an MS in operations research from Case-Western Reserve University, and a PhD in economics from Carnegie Mellon University.

**GEORGE P. SHULTZ** is the Thomas W. and Susan B. Ford Distinguished Fellow at the Hoover Institution. Among many other senior government and private sector roles, he served as secretary of labor in 1969 and 1970, director of the Office of Management and Budget from 1970 to 1972, and secretary of the treasury from 1972 to 1974. He was sworn in on July 16, 1982, as the sixtieth U.S. secretary of state and served until January 20, 1989. In January 1989, he was awarded the Medal of Freedom, the nation's highest civilian honor. Shultz rejoined Stanford University in 1989 as the Jack Steele Parker Professor of International Economics at the Graduate School of Business and as a distinguished fellow at the Hoover Institution. Shultz is the Advisory Council chair of the Precourt Institute for Energy Efficiency at Stanford, chair of the MIT Energy Initiative External Advisory Board, and chair of the Hoover Institution Task Force on Energy Policy. He is a distinguished fellow of the American Economic Association.

**JOHN B. TAYLOR** is the George P. Shultz Senior Fellow in Economics at the Hoover Institution and the Mary and Robert Raymond Professor of Economics at Stanford University. He is an award-winning teacher and researcher, specializing in macroeconomics, international economics, and monetary policy. Among his other roles in public service, he served as a senior economist (1976–77) and as a member (1989–91) of the President's Council of

Economic Advisers and as undersecretary of the treasury for international affairs (2001–5). His book *Getting Off Track: How Government Actions and Interventions Caused, Prolonged, and Worsened the Financial Crisis* was one of the first on the financial crisis; he has since followed up with two books on preventing future crises, coediting *The Road ahead for the Fed* and *Ending Government Bailouts As We Know Them,* in which leading experts examine and debate proposals for financial reform and exit strategies. Before joining the Stanford faculty in 1984, Taylor held positions as a professor of economics at Princeton University and Columbia University. He received a BA in economics summa cum laude from Princeton and a PhD in economics from Stanford University in 1973.

**IAN J. WRIGHT** is a third-year PhD student in the Department of Economics at Stanford University. His research focuses on both theoretical and empirical work pertaining to financial markets. Currently he is studying the dynamics of corporate lending markets, how social interactions influence speculative behavior, and models of the term structure of interest rates. As an undergraduate, Wright attended Brigham Young University, where he earned a bachelor's degree in mathematics and economics and graduated with the Orson Pratt Prize in 2009. He is also a recipient of the Shultz Graduate Student Fellowship in Economic Policy, and a consultant for Credit Sesame, Inc., where he works on interest rate forecasting.

*About the Hoover Institution's*

# Working Group on Economic Policy

**The Working Group on Economic Policy** brings together experts on economic and financial policy at the Hoover Institution to study key developments in the U.S. and global economies, examine their interactions, and develop specific policy proposals.

For twenty-five years starting in the early 1980s, the United States economy experienced an unprecedented economic boom. Economic expansions were stronger and longer than in the past. Recessions were shorter, shallower, and less frequent. GDP doubled and household net worth increased by 250 percent in real terms. Forty-seven million jobs were created.

This quarter-century boom strengthened as its length increased. Productivity growth surged by one full percentage point per year in the United States, creating an additional $9 trillion of goods and services that would never have existed. And the long boom went global with emerging market countries from Asia to Latin America to Africa experiencing the enormous improvements in both economic growth and economic stability.

Economic policies that place greater reliance on the principles of free markets, price stability, and flexibility have been the key to these successes. Recently, however, several powerful new economic forces have begun to change the economic landscape, and these principles are being challenged with far-reaching implications for U.S. economic policy, both domestic and international. A financial crisis flared up in 2007 and turned into a severe panic in 2008, leading to the Great Recession. How we interpret and react to these forces—and in particular whether proven policy principles prevail going forward—will determine whether strong economic growth and stability returns and again continues to spread and improve more people's lives or whether the economy stalls and stagnates.

Our Working Group organizes seminars and conferences, prepares policy papers and other publications, and serves as a resource for policy-makers and interested members of the public.

## Working Group on Economic Policy

Many of the writings associated with this Working Group will be published by the Hoover Institution Press or other publishers. Materials published to date, or in production, are listed below. Books that are part of the Working Group on Economic Policy's *Resolution Project* are marked with an asterisk.

# Index

(f = figure, t = table, n = footnote)